Bellevue
Literary
Review

*A journal of humanity
and human experience*

Volume 3, Number 1, Spring 2003
Department of Medicine
New York University School of Medicine
www.BLReview.org

The *Bellevue Literary Review* is published twice a year by the Department of Medicine at New York University School of Medicine.

The Editors invite submissions of previously unpublished works of fiction, nonfiction, and poetry that touch upon relationships to the human body, illness, health, and healing. We encourage creative interpretation of these themes. Full guidelines can be found at www.BLReview.org. Please address all correspondence to *Bellevue Literary Review*, Department of Medicine, NYU School of Medicine, 550 First Avenue OBV-612, NY, NY 10016.

Subscriptions: 1 year: $12
              3 years: $30

The Editorial Staff of the *Bellevue Literary Review* expresses its deep appreciation to the following people who have assisted with editorial review: Toby Leah Bochan, Serena Fox, Harriet Geller, Heather Genovese, Midge Goldberg, Harvey Greenberg, Jackie Keer, April Krassner, Carolyn Krupp, Florence Kugel, George Lipkin, Nikki Moustaki, Anna Reisman, Ginny Wiehardt, and Carol Zoref. We also thank Herb Leventer of the NYU Medical Bookstore and Lorinda Klein of Bellevue Public Affairs for their assistance

The Editors would especially like to acknowledge support and encouragment from David Watts of the Squaw Valley Community of Writers, Michael Collier of the Bread Loaf Writers' Conference, Amber Dorko Stopper of NightRally Magazine, and the Ragdale Foundation.

Cover Note: Bellevue chest physicians review an X-ray of a TB patient, circa 1932. The insignia on the jacket of the physician—the Cross of Lorraine—was the symbol of the NY Lung Association. The presence of female physicians was somewhat unusual for its time. Dr. James Alexander Miller, founder of the Bellevue Chest Service, was the personal physician to the brother of New York City Mayor Jimmy Walker, and apparently cured him of TB. As a result, the Mayor lobbied City Council to provide funds for the Bellevue Chest Service, which was housed in the C&D building. This building is still part of Bellevue Hospital today. Courtesy of Bellevue Hospital Archives: Chest Collection. (Other photos on pages 8, 12, 13, 23, 42, 53, 92, 112, 126, 149.)

Bellevue Literary Review

A journal of humanity and human experience

Danielle Ofri   *Editor-in-Chief*

Ronna Wineberg   *Fiction Editor*
Jerome Lowenstein   *Nonfiction Editor*

Roxanna Font   *Poetry Editor*
Donna Baier Stein   *Poetry Editor*

Martin J. Blaser   *Publisher*

Editorial Board

Nadia Ahmad
Felice Aull
David Baldwin
Carol Berman
Denitza Blagev
Joseph Cady
Rafael Campo
Rita Charon

Bill Cole
Tony Dajer
Ruth Danon
Stuart Dickerman
Kate Falvey
Will Grossman
Itzhak Kronzon
Michael A. LaCombe
Lois Lowenstein

Michael Pillinger
Norman Posner
Marc Rothman
Marc Seigel
Abraham Verghese
Gerald Weissmann
David Zimmerman
Abigail Zuger

Troi Santos   *Graphic Designer*
Benjamin Akman   *Web Designer*
Doris Milman   *Copy Editor*

Stacy Bodziak   *Coordinating Manager*
Lucy Cribben   *Department Administrator*
Elsa Nunez, Liz Peterson   *Office Associates*
Pearl Kan, Lisbeth Kaufman,   *Interns*
Nichola Tucker

Contents

Volume 3, Number 1, Spring 2003

Fiction

Nonfiction

Poetry

Foreword

Tuberculosis has woven its way through the arts as the prototype of the romantic illness. In such classics as *The Magic Mountain* and *La Bohème*, TB serves as a medium for spirituality, love, and self-reflection. At Bellevue Hospital, TB is far less romantic, more routinely associated with bloody coughs, raging fevers, and wasting away, than it is with artistic delicacy. The Bellevue Chest Service opened in 1903 to deal with the tuberculosis epidemic of the time, introducing many significant new medical treatments. The epidemic waned, but the Chest Service never closed, and indeed was ready with open doors when tuberculosis re-emerged with a vengeance in the 1980s on the coattails of HIV, homelessness, and drug addiction.

This year marks the centennial of the Bellevue Chest Service and the *Bellevue Literary Review* is delighted to honor it with a number of historical photographs scattered through our text, as well as an essay by Joan Reibman about the clinical experience of the Chest Service then and now. And in the tradition of Mann and Puccini, the *BLR* is pleased to publish *A Room With No Door*, Megan Corazza's haunting story of TB infecting a poor Nepalese family.

In the Spring 2003 *BLR,* we also explore writing inspired by other illnesses, some with quite younger literary pedigrees than tuberculosis. Eisenmenger's disease, a congenital heart condition, is the illness—or perhaps the mark of health—against which all other lives are necessarily measured, in the delightful saga *My Blue Cousin* by Itzhak Kronzon. We also present two provocative works on organ donation, from the perspective of would-be donors contemplating the profound issue of sacrificing their own body parts to save the lives of others. In H. L. McNaugher's essay *Imminence*, the author wonders if she, now of legal age, will be called upon to donate a kidney to her mother, since the first donated kidney is failing. In Susan Ito's story *The Liver Nephew*, issues of transplantation are jumbled with cultural expectations, family duties, and the clash of generations.

Psychiatric illnesses also provide potent inspiration for writers. Sheila Kohler, in her intricately rendered story *The Mask*, observes a young psychiatrist facing the reality of his own life, stirred by his meeting with a challenging patient and an older physician. In *MacNamara's Ghost*, by Steve Fayer, the recollections of a psychiatric patient force his brother to re-think the premises of their lives. *Mood Swings*, a poem by Erica Funkhouser, provides a piercingly accurate description of emotional instability.

Orthodox and unorthodox medical treatments often rub against each other in ways that offer literary inspiration. *Ask Him If He Knows Jesus* is Clarence Smith's tale of an open-minded but still skeptical medical student on a church-sponsored medical mission in Venezuela. Sandra Kohler's poem *The Cure* explores the desperate need to heal body and soul. In *wifebeat*, Michael Casey examines the chilling prospect of no cure.

The *BLR* is delighted to present three prose-poems by Pulitzer Prize-winner James Tate. In a lyrical romp through humanity, Tate manages to cover birth, death, and the Easter bunny with uncanny wit and insight.

Several stories in the *BLR* examine sexuality. In Abraham Verghese's poignant story, *If Brains Was Gas*, a thirteen-year-old girl explores life with her irrepressible but troubled uncle. In *Youthful Acts of Charity*, Marylee MacDonald takes her Rubenesque fifty-five-year-old protagonist on an adventure with a young Turkish tour guide.

The lives of doctors and their families take center stage in two stories. David Milofsky's *Differential Diagnosis* features a neurologist debating the possible causes of her patient's symptoms and her own troubled marriage. In *Home Free*, Daniel Bryant's protagonist is a stay-at-home father balancing the challenges of raising a toddler and being a writer, while his wife struggles through her residency training.

This is the fourth issue of the *Bellevue Literary Review*. We are pleased to offer a widening range of writing about the human condition. The prism of health and healing, illness and disease, and the human body and mind offer vast potential for stimulating discourse. The *Contributors' Notes* highlights the outstanding assemblage of authors who have helped the *Bellevue Literary Review* become a unique voice in literature and in medicine.

Danielle Ofri, MD, PhD
Editor-in-Chief

Bellevue Hospital Tuberculosis ward, male section, circa 1907. Courtesy of Bellevue Hospital Archives: Chest Collection.

Snapshots of Bellevue

The Bellevue Chest Service, 1903-2003
Joan Reibman

For the resident assigned to the Chest Service of Bellevue Hospital in 2003, the month promises misery: no interns, no friends, and exposure to potentially deadly strains of tuberculosis. Chances are, the resident has never heard of Andre Cournand or Dickinson Richards, who, laboring in the Chest Physiology lab, inserted a ureteral catheter into the right heart, winning them a Nobel Prize. Nor of James Alexander Miller, whose comprehensive focus on tuberculosis led to the Chest Service's founding in 1903. The resident's worries are more pressing: how many admissions will there be, how many TB patients will be involuntarily detained on the service, will the social worker find place-ment for the homeless patients. In the daily crush, who can afford to remember that the Bellevue Chest Service has been, and remains, for the unlucky of the world, the refuge of last resort?

The first stop in daily rounds: a young college student, eager to begin her studies but delayed by the onset of a cough and chest pain. She is wearing a pink nightgown covered by a matching bathrobe. On her Formica bedside stand, there are flowers and a balloon dangling off a stick; "Get Well Soon," it declares. Her family has brought her food; she will not have to eat the dried curds of egg splattered over her breakfast tray, the aftermath of a careless delivery. When the dreaded word "TB" is mentioned, she will cry, not com-prehending how she could have become so unclean, and will not know how to explain to family, to friends. She will become even more upset when the ques-tion of an HIV test is broached. The reassurance, the explanations, the dis-cussion of medications passes over her; she has heard only "TB" and "HIV."

From there, it's on to 7 West. The team passes the guard who glances up, legs on the desk, belly bulging over the tightly-belted uniform, every daily rag in reach; "Cops Had To Shoot!" blares The Post. This is the locked ward, aimed mostly at the miscreants who have tried to skip their daily treatment, having tired of all their pills and visits to a health worker. Hunted out by the Department of Health, they have been returned to the Chest Service and com-mitted to the seventh circle. Some are angry, call their lawyers, sit on their beds chaotic with sheaths of disordered papers demanding their release. Others are resigned, lie in bed staring at the ceiling, the empty walls, the TV, their heads on plastic pillows which escape the graying synthetic cases.

There is the fumbling for masks as the group crowds into room 7W32, jostling through the double-doored passage, built to stem the flow of mycobacteria. A cachectic Tibetan man cowers in his bed, his sheets in turmoil. He speaks no English and nods uncomprehendingly as masked residents prod his chest. His protruding ribs prevent the stethoscopes from lying flat. There's no mystery to his diagnosis: multiple-drug resistant TB, for which he is receiving multiple medicines: PAS, Ethionamide, Levoquin, Capreomycin. There are the daily intramuscular injections, though little muscle can be found. He can tolerate all of this. What he cannot tolerate is the guard, who, when he knocked on the patient's door, caused him to barricade himself in his room, crazed with memories of torture in China. Now even the residents, with their duck-billed masks, evoke fear. For days he will remain mute, unable to communicate even to the one nurse who speaks his language.

In the room across the hall, the mood is very different. A young, strapping Russian is looking pleased. *"Da,"* he says, nodding to everyone. Using all his family's savings, he had flown to New York, unmasked, on a commercial airline. Via the Brooklyn network, he landed in Bellevue. Befriended by a Russian-speaking social worker, he learns that his drug resistant TB may require months in isolation. No problem; in Russia, he would be left to die. Someone has provided him with a small electronic translator and with glee, he insists that his doctors stay and translate. They shift uneasily to the back wall; with visions of aerosolized mycobacteria, their goal is to extricate themselves from his UV-lit room as quickly as they can.

Their rounds completed, the young residents shed their masks with relief. They may not know that their predecessors, fifty years earlier, faced an almost one-in-five chance of contracting TB. Walker Percy started as a Bellevue resident, only to become a patient on the Chest Service. The intensity of his isolation gave him a second life writing the novels *The Moviegoer* and *Love in the Ruins*, winning him acclaim. Other writers had preceded him; in the 1930's, when most hospitals in America were segregated, Wallace Thurman, the noted chronicler of the Harlem Renaissance, was treated on these wards. It was consistent with the mission of Bellevue; in the early photos, there are black patients along with the whites. One can follow the photos backward in time: there's the Bellevue boat, the sick on deck-chairs, wrapped in blankets, taking the "fresh air cure" in New York's East River. There's the open ward: the neatly made beds, all in a row. The nurses look straight at the camera, their pinafores gleaming white, their hair neatly tied back under starched hats. In the clinic waiting room, row upon row of the sick patiently await their turn. When Miller opened the Bellevue Chest Service in 1903, Europe's poorest were flooding Ellis Island at an unprecedented pace. The order of his clinic was a heroic reply to the chaos that surrounded him.

Today, the uniforms are less prim, the clinic benches long since replaced by a haphazard collection of chairs, and the patients are from Tibet, Bangladesh, Kazakhstan, Ecuador, Senegal, Yemen. Those harried residents on the Chest Ward are too busy, right now, to worry about their place in history. But hopefully one day they'll look back and know that they were, for that month, part of Miller's heroic reply. When Walker Percy called Bellevue his "great good fortune," he meant that TB had driven him to his life's calling as a writer. For most who pass through Bellevue now, their great good fortune is that a hundred years have not altered the mission of the Chest Service: it is still, for the world's afflicted, a place of hope. ❧

General Dispensary, Bellevue Chest Clinic waiting room, circa 1909. Courtesy of Bellevue Hospital Archives: Chest Collection.

TB patients on the deck of the Southfield Ferry, with Bellevue in the background, circa 1908. The Southfield Ferry was a retired Staten Island Ferry purchased by the Bellevue Auxiliary in 1908 for day treatment of TB, and was moored in the East River. This ferry exploded in 1918 from a boiler accident, and was replaced by another ferry referred to as the Day Camp Boat. Courtesy of Bellevue Hospital Archives: Chest Collection.

If Brains Was Gas

Abraham Verghese

I turned thirteen that week. I assumed that it came with some new liberties, but no one had specifically said so, and I was too uncertain to ask. Still, the night after my birthday, Elmo and me made plans to go out. I washed and conditioned my hair when I got home from school, then dried it and combed it out. Usually I wore my hair in a French Braid, but for that evening I left it loose. When I looked over my shoulder into the mirror, I liked the way my hair reached to my low back.

I came out to the living room and sat on the edge of an armchair. My uncle, J.R., lay on the sofa where he had flopped down as soon as he came home from work, his jacket and boots still on, watching an *Andy Griffith* rerun. Mamaw—my grandmother—was sitting on her recliner, a cigarette sagging on her lips, the smoke above her head looking like the blurb of a cartoon, her hands busy with her puzzles. She glanced up at me and I knew she had me figured out. I had been about to ask Mamaw for permission to go out, but now I pretended to have come out of my bedroom to watch TV.

Mamaw let off a resonant fart and then settled back into the recliner, as if she were momentarily airborne.

"Sheba, Sheba," Mamaw grumbled looking round her chair, but Sheba was in the kennel behind the house and could not be blamed for this one. J.R. and I exchanged glances; "power farts" was what J.R. called them and he claimed they were the cause of the trailer being so loose on its foundation and the brick skirting starting to come loose. He wrinkled his nose, and pushed his front teeth halfway out his mouth. A laugh—though it sounded more like a hiccup—escaped me; I couldn't help myself.

Mamaw glared at me. "Missy, I guess you done done all your homework? Or ain't you got none again?"

"Mamaw!" I said, knowing I had just blown my chance of going out, "It was J.R.! He made me laugh. He pushed his teeth out!"

"Junior Hankins!" She put down her puzzle. "Tell me, son, why did I pay an arm and a leg to have your jaw fixed so it wouldn't stick out like a lantern? For you to scare people half to death?"

J.R., not looking at her, raised off the sofa and leaned towards the TV as though something of the gravest importance had caught his attention: Bill

Gatton of Gatton Ford-Hyundai-Mazda was dressed as an Arab and talking about a tent sale. Mamaw's eyes bored into J.R., but his own eyes became little slits as he studied the TV and tapped his temple with a thoughtful finger; he nodded as he listened to Arab Bill. I tensed up. Now I was in trouble with both of them.

"Thirty-one year old and act like a four year old," was all Mamaw said. She turned back to her puzzle. J.R. kept his eyes on the TV. I had been holding my breath, and now I let it out. There was a step I felt I was missing, rules that no one had explained to me.

In a minute J.R. caught my eye and he did it again: his upper lip bulged, became pale as it stretched, then turned out to reveal the denture. It slid out like the head of a snail, came to a rest perching on his chin, pink, wet, and in a perpetual leer. When I was a baby, J.R. had stuck his teeth out at me and made me terrified of all men—this is what Mamaw told me—and I was two years old before I would go near my father who left soon after anyway. My mother (J.R.'s only sister) had disappeared soon after. Mamaw had raised me. J.R. had lived with us ever since I could remember. When he married Onesta, she joined us, which I always thought was one too many people to be living decently in a double-wide, but nobody had asked for my opinion.

"Missy," J.R. said, heaving off the sofa, "let's you and I go to Kmart. I need motor oil. Just run out." He shook his key chain with the big-boobed mermaid. Jingle, Jingle, Jingle.

"She ain't going to Kmart or nowheres this time of night," Mamaw said without looking up from her puzzle.

"Mamaw!" I said, sure that my date with Elmo was off, but hoping at least I would get to go with J.R.

"Ma," J.R. said, "we're going to Kmart, and she is plenty old enough to go out, and it's only seven-thirty, and Onesta ain't back from work yet, and supper ain't ready, so quit your whining, and think about dining…" He walked over behind her and bent over and kissed Mamaw noisily on the side of her face. When he raised up, he grimaced for my benefit, as if he had slammed into the stink wall behind her recliner.

My coat was on, my pocketbook was on my shoulder, and I was shining the door knob with my sleeve, avoiding Mamaw's eyes, waiting for J.R., hoping Mamaw would say nothing to stop me.

I climbed into J.R.'s pickup and shut the door. "Lock and load," he said, just as the engine came to life. With one fluid, practiced motion—I had never seen anyone else do this—J.R. flipped the heater on defrost, the fan on high, the radio on WJHW 104 FM, the headlights on high-beam, the parking brake off, the gear in reverse, pushed the cigarette lighter in, let the clutch out, and it seemed we were rolling before the 351 big block completed its first cycle. J.R. looked at me while he did all this, to show me that he did this entirely by feel and because he knew I appreciated this sort of talent. Elmo couldn't do nothing like that.

Sitting Big-Foot high in that cab, the night dark around us, the unlit gravel road crunching beneath our wheels, only the instrument lights glowing, I felt we were in the cockpit of our private plane, off on a secret mission. Only J.R. could make me feel this way. With his short beard growing high on his cheekbones, his close-set blue eyes that always made it seem as if he could see right through me, and the brown hair parted in the middle and longish like Jesus Christ, I thought he was the handsomest and sexiest man I knew. Kind of like the Alabama lead singer, though J.R. had done that look first. It was strange how I could be with Elmo, him smelling of hot water and soap, the Pinto giving off Pine Sol fumes, ten-dollars in Elmo's pocket to burn, but never feel as good as I did with J.R.

At the first traffic light within the city limits, J.R. pulled up next to an old couple in a blue sedan and yelled through closed windows, "Hey Stupid!" and then stared straight ahead. The old man, thinking he heard something, looked up at us. J.R. turned to the old man as if to say 'What in the hell are you looking at?' The old man looked away. I wished I had peed before we left the house.

We pulled into Kmart and parked in a handicapped spot. A lady with giant curlers under her scarf and a shopping cart half-full of Alpo and paper towels, scowled at us. J.R. put on a limp and let one hand curl up in front of his chest, spastic-like, and stumbled in her direction. She muttered and her little steps got faster and faster as she tried to skirt J.R. When J.R. stepped on the rubber mat and the door swung open, he was miraculously healed. His back straightened, his arm unfolded, his chin was held high, and he strode in as if he were Stonewall Jackson in Levi's, boots, and black bomber jacket. And he knew I was behind him, watching.

We walked the aisles; I looked at the shelves while J.R. looked at the women. The place was full and Christmas music was still playing. The customers seemed relaxed and happy, while the store clerks looked harried. J.R. asked a brunette with a "Let Me Help You" button whether condoms were sold in the hardware section. She gobbled and her eyes got goldfish big before she fled. "Happy New Year," J.R. called after her.

My heart was racing. Was it just coincidence that he asked about condoms? I started to check my purse, and then snapped it shut when I remembered the cameras above. They might think I was shoplifting. The speaker above my head blared "Attention Kmart Shoppers," and J.R. stopped in mid-step and yelled: "Yo!"

In Household Furnishings, J.R. sneezed his "accshit" sneeze. People stared around aisles and between shelves. J.R. sneezed again, a double sneeze: "accshit, aaaacshit," leaving no doubts. He pushed his teeth out at an old lady who seemed hypnotized by him. I stood there. I knew people looked at me and thought I was J.R.'s girl. There was nothing I could do about that, and besides, it made me feel good. I wondered if J.R. felt the same way.

In the parking lot we ran into a guy J.R. knew. J.R. was fixing to buy dope. The guy's hair was extra long and he pushed it behind his ears, first one side then the other. His fingers had gnawed-down nails with clear polish on them and he had letters tattooed in the webs between his fingers. I studied his face to see if he felt stupid about any of this. I heard J.R. say, "Don't worry about her. She's fine."

We went to the guy's car and drove to the far end of the parking lot, near the dumpster. He and J.R. lit up a fat joint and passed it back and forth, ignoring me. I sat in the back seat, looking out the side window, trying to breathe in as much of the car air as I could without drawing attention to myself. When they were ready to leave the car, I stepped out and almost fell on my face, grabbing the door. Back in the pickup, J.R. said, "You high, Squirt? I seen you trying to suck up all the air in the car."

I shook my head, trying to look bored, but I was smiling and could not control it. I closed my eyes and leaned my head to one side. This was my test to see if I was high: if I was, my head would feel like a large boulder rolling down the side of a mountain. It felt that way now in J.R.'s pickup.

Elmo pulled in to Kmart just as we were pulling out. I made J.R. stop and roll down the window. I leaned over J.R. to hear Elmo. Elmo stuck his head out and twisted it up to talk to me. He had gone to my house looking for me, he said.

"I'm with J.R., tonight," I replied, leaning against J.R., squishing him.

"So?" Elmo said. But his voice lost confidence. "He's your uncle, right?"

"Damn!" J.R. said to Elmo, "you really *should* go to college. Missy, he is *not* as dumb as he looks." Traffic was backing up behind Elmo. A car honked and even though it was dark, I knew Elmo's face was turning beet-red. We pulled away.

"*If brains was gas,*" J.R. began, and I joined in, "*Elmo wouldn't have enough to prime a piss-ant's go-cart around a Cheerio.*" When we reached "Cheerio" we were both rolling with laughter. I felt sorry for Elmo but I couldn't stop laughing. Everyone in passing cars knew we were stoned. They were looking at us. Everyone knew. I was glad we were heading home.

J.R. looked down at a couple in a Corvette next to us at a traffic light. "Holy mackerel, Missy," he said, "look at the cock-box on that young'un."

I didn't get a good look at the woman, just an impression of long legs and lipstick. "Fuck her, buddy. *I* did," J.R. shouted

"What's a cock-box, J.R.?" I asked for no reason, thinking of how Elmo squirmed when I had wanted to study his hard-on. Elmo hadn't minded if I touched it, but he didn't want me to *look*.

"You *know* damn well what a cock-box is, Squirt. Get fresh with me and I'll tell Mamaw all about you smoking dope and fumbling with Elmo in the burley shed."

I felt my face turn red. J.R. laughed his 'Hee-Haw' laugh and said "Fumblefumblefumblefumble," his lips a'splutter. I slapped at him. He can read my mind, I thought. The lollipop condom, floating in its juices and burning a hole in my pocketbook—he knows. Since I got the condom, I hadn't been with Elmo. Mamaw, and then J.R., had seen to it.

"I *control* Elmo," I said to J.R. for no particular reason. "That's what I like about him. *I control him.*"

J.R. looked at me strangely. "Control this," he said to me, sticking his middle finger in the air. I tried to break his finger, but my laughter made me a poor enforcer.

"You know something, Squirt," J.R. said in the pickup, as we rode back, stoned, from our Kmart motor oil mission, "I have found my *true* love. I have found the person who can satisfy me sexually, spiritually, and in every other way."

"Yeah, I like Onesta too," I said, lying through my teeth.

"Hell with Onesta. I don't mean Onesta."

Does he mean me? My mind worked like slow treacle and no words came out. I felt tingly all over. My face was burning. I knew in the last year I had blossomed. My tits in profile were every bit as good as Cher's. And J.R. had seen me once when I had put on make-up and heels when Mamaw was out shopping, and he had given me a wolf whistle. I didn't have slut eyes like Daisy Nunley, I didn't have knockers like Juanita Clayber, I didn't have a brother who pimped for me like Wanda Pearson. But I guess I had *something*, I knew that, and it was a good feeling. Mamaw knew it too and it made Mamaw extra surly and made her keep close tabs on me, and warn me about "turning out like your dang-fool mother."

"I don't know why I am telling you this, Squirt," J.R. continued, "but I sure as hell don't mean Onesta."

My stomach tightened. I felt like I had been in a car like this before and some other man said these same words. I looked around at the field whizzing by. I told myself: *I must remember this moment clearly.* I focused on a field on my side of the car, but the field had no boundary and as we drove by it went on forever.

"Me?" I blurted out. "Do you mean me?"

J.R. laughed for a long time. He looked at me with admiration, as if he didn't know I could be so funny. A little girl inside me began to weep, even though I knew I should be relieved.

"Someone else, Squirt. Not you. The love of my life. The reason for my living," he said.

Did this mean J.R. would leave home, I wondered. The thought of being alone with Mamaw—without J.R. or Onesta—crossed my mind and was painful. I thought of Onesta: Onesta from Oneida, raven-haired Onesta, pretty Onesta, dumb-as-a-coal-bucket Onesta. Yet, J.R. had always acted like he knew what he wanted from Onesta. And what she was—pretty and dumb—was exactly what he had wanted.

I found myself speaking: "What the hell do you get married for in the first place? If you're just going to…" I was surprised at the half-sob in my voice. I turned away so he couldn't see my face.

J.R. gave this careful consideration. "When I met Onesta, '*This is it*,' I said. 'This is it.' So I got married."

"Well you were dumb as shit for not knowing better." The look of surprise on J.R.'s face reminded me of Elmo's face in the parking lot. "*This is it*, you said?" I continued, taunting J.R. "*This is it*? So what the hell happened? What happened to, *This is it*?" A part of me felt as if I were Onesta.

"Things happen," I heard J.R. say. "That feeling you have when you marry someone, when you love someone…it's great for a while, but it doesn't last. I met someone else now, Missy. She gives me that feeling again. It feels so good, Squirt. I can't control it."

"Same thing can happen again, J.R." I said softly.

He didn't say anything for a while. We were into fog again and he slowed the pickup. He lit up a fat roach that had been in his pocket and took in a deep drag. His eyes bugged out. "Hell, *I* know that," he said between his teeth, holding the smoke in. I snatched the roach from him. The pickup swerved as he tried to get it back. I leaned against my door, out of his reach, my feet raised, ready to kick him in the face. He backed off. I took deep leisurely drags, holding them in as long as I could.

"You're something else, Missy," he said. Now, give that back…"

"Fuck you, Uncle," I said. "Fuck you, you big dummy. You can be so…funny, so…brave. But you're a *stupid shit* on top of that."

I saw him flinch. He got serious, his eyes mournful, and I sat up and was just about to say I was sorry when he stuck his teeth out. I threw a punch at him, but he slipped it and it buried itself in the shoulder part of his jacket. He held his fist out, ready to bust me if I tried to hit him again. He was bobbing on the seat now, like Ali, jiggling his eyebrows up and down, a big grin on his face, stealing glances at the road, waiting for me to punch. "The greatest of *all* time!" he said. I was still glad I didn't ride with Elmo.

When we came down our driveway it was almost eight o'clock. A car without lights came roaring out of the driveway and took off up the hill. I looked back and could see it was a Chevy hardtop.

"Who the fuck . . .," I said.

I didn't recognize it, but J.R. seemed to and was subdued. I could see that the car had stopped near the main road and now it waited, the engine running. Onesta's car was in the yard. J.R. sat in the pickup for a while and I waited with him. Something told me not to open my mouth.

J.R. entered the trailer through the kitchen door and I followed. Mamaw and Onesta were at the kitchen table, facing each other, smoking. Onesta's eyes were red. Mamaw had her bottle of Jack Daniel's on the table and was sucking on ice chips at the bottom of her glass. She looked mad. Maybe she had found out about the condom. Maybe Elmo came back and spilled the beans. Maybe the pickup truck was bugged. Maybe that car was the FBI and we were going to the slammer.

When Mamaw opened her mouth I thought she would ask me why my eyes were red. But she was looking right through me at J.R.

"It's about time you brought the young'un home," Mamaw said softly.

"Missy, sweetheart, would you go to your room?" Onesta said, not looking at me, but staring at the table.

"What are you, her mother?" J.R. asked. His voice sounded funny.

Mamaw hissed: "What are you, her father?"

"Could be," said J.R., looking at Onesta.

Mamaw reached up and slapped J.R. across the cheek. The anger in her eyes was like nothing I had ever seen. My body felt heavy; I could not move.

"You tell Mamaw about your girlfriend?" asked Onesta in a quiet, restrained voice.

"*You* tell her, Onesta," he replied, glancing at the door that lead to the living room.

"You tell Mamaw how she's married?"

"She ain't…married," said J.R., a quaver in his voice that gave away his lie. The second hand of the kitchen clock was the loudest sound in the room. We all looked at him. I thought to myself: this is not real, this is not happening. But for the first time since we walked in, it dawned on me that this might have nothing to do with me.

Mamaw grasped J.R.'s shirt, almost fondling it, and slowly pulled him down so his face was inches from hers. She whispered, "Read my lips, dummy. *She* is married. *You* are married. *Her goddamn husband is in the living room waiting to talk to you.*"

"She ain't married," J.R. said. His voice had cracks in it.

The swinging door from the living room opened and a man I had never seen before walked in. I was sure he would have a gun in his hand. I wanted to pee in my pants.

He was squat and carried himself very upright so as not to waste inches. He was wearing a cream shirt, jeans, and black loafers with white socks. He had red hair that was pulled from behind one ear in a sweeping arc to cover his baldness.

"Are you J.R.?" the man asked, pushing his glasses back on his nose. His teeth were even, with spaces between them. They were clearly his own teeth. His eyes were blue and clear.

I stepped away from J.R.

J.R stepped behind Mamaw.

Mamaw sighed, her head bent over the table, and then she ground out her cigarette. J.R. looked around the kitchen—as though seeing it for the first time—and his Adam's apple bounced like a yo-yo. Mamaw poured a big dollop of Jack.

"I am Katherine's husband," the man said.

J.R. seemed about to say something, his hands moved, but no words came out.

"Katherine done told me all about you and her," the man said. "She asked for my forgiveness and I've given it. She done confessed in front of the whole church. God has forgiven her. She confesses of her own free will."

J.R. tried to look at the man while he spoke but could not hold his gaze.

The man continued, his voice rising in pitch, but very clear. "I done forgiven you, too. I don't appreciate what you done to my family but I've forgiven you. I sure hope your wife can do the same."

Onesta began to cry. J.R. tried to glare her down but she was not looking at him, and besides this was not the time for it.

"I will ask that you stay clear of *my* wife. I don't want to see you anywhere around her," the man said.

J.R. looked at the wall behind the man's head. The man turned to go out through the swinging door. He stopped and bowed his head as though about to add something, and then, thinking the better of it, left. We heard the Chevy pull into the driveway and then drive out.

No one spoke in the kitchen.

J.R. took a deep breath as if to compose himself, to ready his explanation.

Onesta took a long sip from Mamaw's glass. Neither Mamaw nor Onesta would look at J.R. He looked at me over their bowed heads. He tried to get the mischief back into his eyes but they appeared shallow and shifty. He tried to smile, but his cheeks were quivering and the smile threatened to degenerate into a sob.

I waited.

J.R.'s eyes pleaded with me.

As if with a will of its own, his denture came pushing out at me—an offering. Under his sad eyes, he gummed the denture. It glistened with saliva. His upper lip was flabby and sunken. It was pathetic, like an old man's nakedness.

Then, in what I think now was the cruelest moment of my life, I yelled at him. "You big dummy!"

Mamaw and Onesta looked up, surprised at my outburst, but I continued, "You big dummy! If brains was gas...you, you..."

I walked out. My eyes were blurry and my feet slipped on the gravel road. I took deep breaths. I took the condom from my purse and ripped its cover off with my teeth. I chewed the condom, tasting the oily lubricant, hearing it squeak as I ground it to a pulp. I felt a calmness, a sense of who I was, a sense of completely inhabiting my body. It was like nothing I had ever experienced. ❧

"Corrective exercises" on grass alongside the Southfield Ferry, circa 1915. Photographer: Jessie Tarbox Beals. Courtesy of Bellevue Hospital Archives: Chest Collection.

The Cure

Sandra Kohler

Waking before dawn at a motel in a strange city
from a dream in which I am exploring its dark
streets, I see the wet umbrella in the bathtub,
remember arriving soaked and clammy from
a drought-ending day's worth of cold rain,
wrapping myself in the bedclothes, drinking wine.
What comes back then are those nights years ago,
in the months after I'd left my husband, when
each day I allowed myself one scotch at bedtime,
as if by a prescription written to let me lie down
alone and sleep, my measure of loneliness answered
by that measure of oblivion, taken neat. A pure ritual:
one drink only, never more, taken without fail.
I was my own physician, patient and understanding:
I knew I'd been broken and needed to heal. Each
night's sleep was anodyne I steeped in—or was it
a placebo keeping my disease at bay? Older, sadder,
happier, I could not treat myself with such decisive
will, the rigid discipline of youth, unbending,
dogmatic. I binge, starve, sleep or wake as terror
and the craving for oblivion wax and wane like tides,
extreme as summer's months of drought, last night's
flooding antidote. Loss, anguish, fear of dying
alone, of living alone: all recur; no cure, no cure.

ॐ

One Summer

Sandra Kohler

i.

We sleep with the windows open wide,
the shades up—no separations
from the night, the world.
Morning the room's no sanctuary,
pervaded with day before we wake:
opaque, gray, unchanging,
summer's fugue of repetition.
It rained before we woke and as
we were waking and now rain is in
the streets, a sound under every car.
A white bird flies across
the evergreens' solid screen.
I am moved by the intricacies of breath,
my heart's extra beat. We sing as a species,
mocking the green densities
of an accepted world, the iron grip
of this season, extremity, stasis.

ii.

When the thunder started last night
we kept playing. It reached us in fragments,
each the music of a bar of lightning
scoring miles of sky. Even the rain
could not end our playing. Others departed,
but we were summer, persistent,
skies that resume their gray deliberation
despite all precipitate interruption.

Only the days have sequence, number, names.
The taste of experience is changed,
salt, a pang of new, not quite bitter
knowledge: something stirring beneath
stale leaves. The body has doors,
won't let us close them, though we long
sometimes for a repression so absolute
it leaves us peaceful, dumb as stones.
Nothing hurts like the new, the raw,
opening, breaking: the loneliness
of space on new skin. We act and act
again. We are reflected by the empty
fields, the still light in the sky.

iii.

The wind this morning: moist, fresh,
a mute wish for renewal.
It begins in the tropical latitudes,
turbulent lava. It blows itself out
over ocean, cooling as it sweeps, gathering
moisture, the breath of trees, faint
exhalation of green stems in marshes
thick with standing waters.

iv.

The sudden silence is not a space
I move into but a space
that descends, rain of another sky,
lingers like smoke, fragrance.
Our memories are not like this:
thin attenuated traces of what once
had body, but a brief return
to full being,
the shock of what was present again.
Don't ask how: the door opens.

v.

The morning already wears a stain,
a mask of heat: midsummer haze.
Outside in the street a man coughs
into the Sunday hush. It resumes,
a pond composing itself. A plane
disturbs the sky, the broken thunder
of its pulse travelling the horizon.
A word with rise in it, a delicate
aroused word: horizon. A dog barks
in the backyard, insistent messenger
whose voice I can't decipher.
Something in my body stirs and turns.
The dog is probably chained as most
of us are, by probability. The spirit
and the flesh approach each other,
with only an "I" to bind them.
I am no longer sure what story I am
telling but its ground is summer.

ॐ

My Blue Cousin

Itzhak Kronzon

My Aunt Sonia's daughter Bella was born blue. Based on the letters we received from Russia, we, in Israel, understood that she suffered from a heart defect—the dreaded Eisenmenger's Disease. Father read about the disease in *Meyer's Lexicon*, a 16-volume illustrated encyclopedia in German that he'd won in a card game many years ago while serving in the Latvian Air Force. He drew for us a sort of road map of the heart of my blue cousin, whom we had never met, and gave us a complicated explanation, complete with arrows, about the hole between the chambers of her heart, and the clean blood that mixed with the dirty blood. We understood very little, and Mother understood even less, but the blue color frightened her. Mother wanted to know how blue her skin was, and pointed at several objects in our apartment that were various shades of blue: the tablecloth, the linen closet, the Chinese picture on the ceramic teacup. Was it this blue? Or was it like this? Father had never seen anyone with Eisenmenger's, and *Meyer's Lexicon* was not illustrated in color, but Father was never at a loss for an answer. He picked up the book of receipts that he wrote out for residents of the building he managed on Jezreel Street in Bat Galim, and extracted a rectangular piece of carbon paper, waved it in our astonished faces, and quietly said, "Like this."

Years have passed, but every time I see a piece of carbon paper, I think of my blue cousin Bella.

My Aunt Sonia—my mother's sister—lived in Riga. She was married to my Uncle Pinchas Yacobowitz, the most important eye doctor in the entire Soviet Latvian republic. Blue Bella had two brothers, Lony and Tony, whom I knew only from a small photograph in which they were both standing, wearing sailor shirts and shorts, playing small violins. Their names were always uttered together, and in nickname form—Lonichka and Tonichka. In my imagination, they were as indelibly linked to one another as Siamese twins, in a faraway, inaccessible cold land.

In 1956, when the Soviet heart specialists admitted they could do nothing more for my blue cousin, the authorities allowed her to seek medical help in England, which we took as a sign that the end was near. In England, she contacted my Uncle Pinchas Yacobowitz's brother, who had settled in Liverpool as a young man, become a diamond merchant, changed his name from Chaim

Yacobowitz to Charles Jacobs, and married a non-Jewish woman with whom he had a daughter, to the consternation of his entire family. Until the daughter was born, Mother said, he would still have been able to get rid of the wife. Charles Jacobs took in his blue niece, and it was from him that our family learned that she had been examined at the hospital on Great Ormond Street in London, which is the finest medical center in the world for congenital heart defects. The doctors there decided that there was nothing they could do for her; at the age of fifteen her fate was sealed. "How does something like this happen?" asked Mother, shooting a half-accusatory look at me, since I was a first-year medical student, and as she saw it, it was only reasonable to assume that the global guild of medical practitioners, to which I now belonged, should be doing something about it. Her look also constituted a defiant challenge to God, who took, as she said, children before their parents—an affront to the world order that He Himself had established.

In 1960, while still in medical school, I got married, and the following year, for the first time in our lives, my wife and I took a trip to Europe, which was supposed to be a combination honeymoon and study trip, as part of a student exchange program. With the modest sum of money that we borrowed, we planned to visit Paris and London, and see the sights every novice tourist is supposed to see. But after the plan was finalized and the tickets were purchased, my mother confronted me, a pained expression on her face. She asked that we not forget, Heaven forbid, to visit my blue cousin Bella, who was living with my uncle's brother, Charles Jacobs in Liverpool. In a voice that was part request, part prophecy, Mother explained to us that my cousin, who was getting bluer and bluer as the days went by, had only a few days left. Bella was also the only daughter of her sister Sonia—since Lonichka and Tonichka were boys—and the close family connection, Mother said, was stronger and more important than any satisfaction a pleasure trip might give. Furthermore, her case was important and of interest to anyone studying medicine.

And so we left Israel for the first time, a prayer on my and my wife's lips that my blue cousin would stay alive until our arrival, a prayer shared by Mother and the entire Israeli branch of our family.

While all the tourists were visiting the British Museum, the Tower of London, and the Royal Zoo, I was making my way through the Underground and the bus stations in an attempt to figure out an inexpensive way of getting to Liverpool. Eventually we boarded a slow bus that took all night and half the next day to get there. It was filled with perspiring, beer-drinking Englishmen, who smoked cigarettes and pipes; our eyes wept and we nearly stopped breathing. We waited at a bus station for an hour or two for another bus out to the suburb, where our Uncle Charles Jacobs was waiting for us—a small, bearded, bald, nervous man. We learned, to our great relief, that while we were in transit from London, Bella's condition had remained unchanged, and that we would meet her in a little while, since she was not at home just now, having gone to the library. The wretched girl, said our uncle's brother, could barely carry her own weight. It was a sort of death into which she was being inexorably and forcibly drawn, making her so blue that she was practically black. There was nothing to do.

We arrived at my uncle's beautiful house. His non-Jewish wife was not home, having gone somewhere (thereby saving us the embarrassment and discomfort of the experience—one we'd never been through before—of meeting a non-Jew who was married to a Jew, and a relative, at that). Also absent was the *momzeira* (bastard) daughter produced by this marriage, who had a double non-Jewish name, something like Mary Louise, as if to emphasize that even if her father was of Jewish descent, even if he was Chaim Yacobowitz before becoming Charles Jacobs, she had nothing in common with Judaism, and observed only the beliefs of her non-Jewish mother. Mary Louise, her father— our uncle's brother—told us, went to a boarding school where the pupils slept on wooden boards instead of mattresses, so that they would learn to properly appreciate what it meant to be able to sleep on a mattress. My uncle's brother was very impressed with this non-Jewish educational logic; he seemed happy to adopt the logic and customs of the non-Jews.

Since there was still some time until my blue cousin Bella returned from the library, we were forced to sit in my uncle's brother's sitting room and listen to his opinions about the Israeli merchants who had cheated him until he swore never to do business again with an Israeli, especially if he was from an Arab country—what the English called a Sephardic Jew. My wife, whose nerves were already frayed from the stress of the long trip and the anticipation of seeing my cousin, broke down in tears at hearing the insult, so much so that my uncle's brother ran to the kitchen to make her a cup of tea, hoping that it would soothe her nerves.

While my uncle's brother was making tea in the kitchen, and my wife was in the bathroom wiping away the tears and washing her face, the door opened and my blue cousin Bella walked in. The poor thing had made a vain attempt to conceal her blueness: she had daubed red lipstick on her lips and was wearing red polish on her fingernails. The blend of colors formed an unusual shade of purple, but I of course knew, and could see, her real color, and hear her labored breathing. I felt as if my own flesh were being torn away—she was the only daughter of my Aunt Sonia, Mother's sister—and I kissed her and nearly burst into tears. My cousin let loose two large tears that flowed down her cheeks and looked blue, reflecting the color of her skin. Then my wife returned back from the bathroom and my uncle's brother from the kitchen, and we sat around and chatted, as if my cousin were not blue, and as if no one could hear the fluttering wings of the angel of death there in the sitting room of the suburban Liverpool home.

We certainly would have stayed longer to spend a few more hours with my soon-to-expire cousin, like a candle down to her few last drops of wax, but we still had a two-day trip back to London, and from there to the airport. As we left, we saw her waving to us through the window, as if she were saying: you're going on your way, but what about me?

When we came back to Israel, Mother was waiting for us at the airport, and the first thing she said was, "Did you see her?" Later, we sat at my parents' home on Geula Street and talked about the visit with my blue cousin Bella. Once again Father brought out his *Meyer's Lexicon*, and I my copy of *Boyd's Pathology*, and together we read the entries on Eisenmenger's Disease. Pulmonary hypertension concurrent with a ventricular septal defect resulting in a shunt from the right side of the heart into the left, leading to hypoxic arterial blood and blue skin—a disease without cure, without hope. Did I decide to specialize in cardiology after learning about my blue cousin Bella's disease?

To Mother's delight, and maybe also her sister Sonia's in Riga, my older brother Shmuel was posted as an emissary in Madrid. In that year, 1962, Bella, my blue cousin, left Liverpool and went to Madrid to enjoy life and spend her final days in that city of joy and music. Practically in tears, Mother told me how my blue cousin was going to dances, and that every dance caused her to faint (like a butterfly attracted to a candle's flame, was how Mother put it). Bella gradually grew closer to my brother and his wife, and soon made herself—and her friends—at home in their house, and whenever she needed a place to rest from her abortions, she chose to do so among her true relatives, her own flesh and blood. (If allowed to progress, each of the pregnancies would have led to her death, her physician warned. My brother relayed this information to me, which I had already learned from the medical literature.) When my brother's term of service abroad was over, he and his wife left Madrid with a heavy heart, not only because they were sorry their stay in Spain was over—they loved Madrid—but also because they felt that their departure left my blue cousin without the care and supervision of relatives who were genuinely concerned for her well-being. (Sometimes she was actually black, my brother said. I already knew about that from the books.)

In 1963, Bella learned that antique Russian icons had both artistic and monetary value. That summer, my blue cousin went to visit—perhaps for the last time—her parents in Riga, a trip that was approved by the authorities, and on her return trip to Madrid smuggled a few icons in her bra. Who would search a sick, short-of-breath young woman whose blue skin color alone would be more than enough to cast a spell of bad luck on the primitives who manned the border crossings. Every summer, for the next ten or fifteen years, my blue cousin Bella went for a visit to Riga and then returned to Madrid; the proceeds of each trip were enough to support her financially all year long, if not longer.

At this point in the story I regretfully digress from my blue cousin Bella and tell something about the other members of her family, Lonichka and Tonichka, my Uncle Pinchas Yacobowitz (brother of Charles Jacobs) and my Aunt Sonia. While my cousin's life was hanging by a thread, Lonichka had become a doctor and Tonichka a lawyer. My Uncle Pinchas Yacobowitz wanted to immigrate to Israel, mostly so that he'd be able to establish more of a connection with his daughter Bella. Following an arduous struggle—well known to anyone who was involved in the immigration of Soviet Jews to Israel—my uncle was finally granted an exit permit, and arrived in Israel with his wife and children.

Due to Bella's poor health, and as she had recently been given government support provided to ailing residents, everyone decided that my blue cousin was best off staying in Madrid. She married there, and also went through a divorce or two. As I recall, her first marriage in 1970 earned her Spanish citizenship, and her second marriage granted Spanish citizenship to another Russian émigré. These, of course, are only minor anecdotes in the immigration and naturalization archives of the Spanish government, and not directly relevant to our story. I myself went with my family to New York in 1971 for my medical residency, which dragged on and on until I eventually stayed there. The diplomas of my Uncle Pinchas Yacobowitz, the greatest eye physician in his homeland, were not recognized in Israel. And so, filled with bitterness, he had to take a lowly position at a local clinic. My Aunt Sonia became a secretary. Lonichka, who wanted to be an eye doctor like his father and live near him in Tel Aviv, was sent to do a residency in orthopedics at some hospital, and Tonichka was on the receiving end of a bit of nepotism wielded by Father (under pressure from Mother) and found work as a lawyer in the legal department of the electric company in Hadera.

The brothers might have continued on in these positions were it not for the State of Israel, which sent a draft notice to Tonichka, who was evidently less than interested in the offer, and soon vanished from the country. My furious father would joke and say, "He asked permission to go to the toilet, and found himself flushed with the shit." My Uncle Pinchas Yacobowitz didn't like the joke, and even hinted to Mother that his son (me, that is) had also left the country. Father went pale and made a fist, and it was only thanks to the women, Sonia and Mother, that an exchange of blows, if not a tragedy, was averted. Father had already had two heart attacks, and Pinchas Yacobowitz suffered from hypertension and high blood cholesterol.

Lonichka also disappeared. The two brothers met up again in Liverpool, through the good offices of their Uncle Charles Jacobs, who helped Tonichka set up a food wholesale business, and helped Lonichka finally become an eye doctor at Victory Hospital, the most prestigious hospital in Liverpool.

I have almost forgotten to mention my cousin Natalia, the daughter of my Uncle Ely—Mother and Sonia's brother. In 1946, uncle Ely and his wife were arrested and accused of attempting to flee Latvia for Israel. They were sentenced to fifteen years exile to Siberia. My cousin Natalia was born in prison and was temporarily adopted by my Aunt Sonia and my Uncle Pinchas Yacobowitz, who raised her as a sister to Bella, Lonichka, and Tonichka. They called her Natalichka.

When Sonia and Pinchas Yacobowitz were able to emigrate to Israel, the Soviet authorities also approved exit papers for my Uncle Ely, his wife Raia and their daughter Natalia, all of whom arrived in Israel at the same time. My cousin Natalia was by then a dentist, and found work in a clinic in Netanya, and would no doubt still be there if she hadn't married a new immigrant from Russia who changed his mind about having headed east after his initial arrival in Vienna. In the meantime, both my Uncle Ely and his wife Raia died in Israel, and their daughter Natalia, together with her husband Boris, returned to Vienna and tried to emigrate to America from there. But the officials in Vienna would only provide aid to those who had arrived for the first time. Only then could a Russian be sent to the U.S. and receive financial support from HIAS— the Hebrew Immigrant Aid Society—and the Jewish community. But Natalia and Boris had arrived in Vienna for the second time, so they were considered Israeli immigrants, and no one would help them. So my cousin Natalia was stuck in Vienna with the refugees for three years, along with her husband and the child who was born in the meantime. They'd left Russia, didn't want Israel, were not wanted in Vienna, and America wouldn't take them in. Finally her husband pretended to be a Hassid and was sent with the family to New York as reinforcements for the Lubavitcher Hassidim. Upon arrival in New York, he shed his costume and became a taxi driver, just like the other Israeli émigrés.

In 1974, after Lonichka and Tonichka had left Israel, my Uncle Pinchas Yacobowitz bought a car, promptly drove it into a big tree, and was killed. His sons were unable to come to his funeral, since they would have been arrested at the airport as army deserters. Natalia, his adopted daughter, was still in limbo in Vienna. To Mother and Father's consternation, my blue cousin Bella flew in from Madrid to attend. Everyone at the funeral wept bitterly, not only for the deceased, but also for his sickly daughter to whom respect for a dead father was even more precious than the mortal danger involved with someone in her condition undertaking such a long journey.

Mother and Father died in 1978, she in the winter and he in the summer. They left this world just as they had lived in it—Mother with doubt, hesitation, and pain, and Father with confidence and abruptness. That same year, my Aunt Sonia was diagnosed with leukemia, went to England to be with her sons, and died a painful death there.

Since their parents died, I no longer called my cousins by the childish nicknames Lonichka and Tonichka, but Lony and Tony, more appropriate names for two adult men whose parents were no longer alive.

My older brother Shmuel, a large, robust man, died suddenly in 1981 at the age of 46. Among the condolence telegrams I found one from my blue cousin Bella in Madrid, who was shocked by the sudden death, as were all of us, but I was afraid that the dreadful news about the death of her beloved cousin might deal a harsh blow to her delicate health.

In 1983, my cousin Lony, who had become the top eye specialist in England, came for a visit to New York. He, of course, called his cousin (and adopted sister) Natalia and her husband Boris, the one-time Lubavitcher Hassid who had become a taxi driver, and also, for the first time in our lives, me, and subsequently visited me at my home in New York. He was a kind-hearted, clever, accomplished man who spoke English with a Liverpool accent through which one still discerned vestiges of a Russian inflection. Lony told me that my cousin Tony (whom I had never met) was doing very well in business, had married, and now went by the name of Anthony Jake in Liverpool. Lony also said that my now-orphaned blue cousin Bella was fighting for her life. She was in serious condition, cousin Lony said, speaking as one physician to another.

In April 1998, I stopped off in England on my way from Israel to New York. I telephoned my cousin Lony, and as always, he was happy to hear my voice. That evening, he said, he would come by my hotel to visit, and would bring Bella, who was in England for tests. So once again I met my blue cousin, thirty-seven years after that first trip to Liverpool, where I'd met her at the home of my uncle's brother Charles Jacobs, who had also died in the meantime. My cousin wept tears that flowed down her cheeks, tears that again looked blue to me. The smuggled icons had made her a wealthy woman, and she had a large house in central Madrid together with her husband who also dealt in icons and rare *objets d'art*, and two Afghan dogs. Her situation was desperate. I knew this from my experience as a professor of cardiology, from the books I had read, and from the articles I myself had written on the subject. Eisenmenger's Disease has no cure, and no hope. ❧

Translated from the Hebrew by Martin Friedlander

Waiting To Hear If You Will Die

Jesse Lee Kercheval

I can't move. I do.
My body a fat, numb pillow
I carry from class to office,
take to bed where I lie
awake all night,
my thoughts as restless
as those dusty sparrows
in fast food parking lots.
Pick up the french fry.
Drop the french fry.
I think: *You can't die/*
Everyone dies.
I think: *You've had a good life/*
I'd rather it were me.

॰

Holy Saturday

James Tate

I came out of the store, and the first thing I saw
was a man in a bunny suit dancing down the sidewalk, handing
out chocolate eggs to everyone. Never take candy from strangers
was the first thing that leapt to mind. I wanted to reach the
car before he caught up with me. He saw this, and took a giant
hop in my direction. "Here, this is for you, Mr. Get-away-as-
fast-as-you-can," he said. "I don't want it," I said. "I'm
allergic to chocolate." He made a fist with his paw and threatened
my nose. "Take it," he said, "you can give it to a child, and
they will thank you." "I don't know any children, and, besides,
how do I know there isn't arsenic in there. I don't know you.
You're a complete stranger to me. You might be an escaped convict,
a child molester, or a murderer." "I'm the Easter bunny, you
asshole. If you can't trust the Easter bunny, you're in pretty
bad shape. Take the egg before I shove it down your throat,"
he said. I grabbed him by the shoulders and threw him up against
my car. The whiskers on his nose were twitching. His long,
floppy ears looked pathetic. "You are about to become a
very wounded bunny," I said. "Maybe we could talk this over, over a
beer or something. What do you say?" the bunny said. A couple
of teenagers had gathered to see what I might do next. They
were excited. I, who've never been in a fight, really wanted
to punch the bunny. But, instead, I dragged him off the car.
I took his basket out of his paw and threw it in a trashcan.
"Now go home and get out of that suit. There's enough crime
in this town without you impersonating the Easter bunny and
handing out suspicious substances to little children," I said.
"I was trying to do a good thing," he said. "I was trying to
bring a little cheer and good will, that's all." "But you've
got a bunny suit on, for god's sake. And you were dancing on
the sidewalk like an idiot. Why should anyone trust you?" I
said. "Let's rip that suit off of him and see who he really is,"
one of the teenagers said. The bunny looked really frightened.

He was half-bent over, as if about to hop. "No," I said, "I
think he's learned his lesson." The boys seemed disappointed,
and I was starting to worry about the safety of the bunny.
"Get in the car," I said to him. "What?" he said. "I said,
get in the car. I'll drive you home." I unlocked the car, and
got into the driver's seat. The bunny seemed confused, but did
as I had said. He told me where he lived, and we drove there
in silence. He lived in a run-down apartment complex. Half
the domestic crime in town took place right there. When I
stopped, he started to open the door. He looked so defeated.
"What do you do, I mean, in real life?" I said. "I'm unemployed
right now," he said. "Every time I get a job, the place closes
down. It's like I'm the kiss of death." Hearing this from a
raggedy-assed Easter bunny should have been funny, but it wasn't.
It nearly broke my heart. "I'm sorry I ruined your day. Honestly,
I don't know what came over me. Maybe I was envious of your
happiness," I said. "That's what's great about the bunny suit,"
he said, "no one can see your tears. Thanks for the ride. After
nearly killing me, you saved my life. Makes a perfect story.
Unfortunately, I've got no one to tell it to." He got out of
the car and started hopping across the little, gravelly yard.
I never even saw his face or got his name.

&

Kingdom Come

James Tate

One night, after dinner, Amy announced to me that she
was pregnant. In our three years of marriage, we had never
even mentioned children, so, in my shock, I had to sort of
fake my response, until I could figure out how I really felt.
"That's so great, Amy," I said. "We're going to be parents.
You've made me the happiest man in the world." "It's kind of
a surprise, though, isn't it? I mean, it wasn't as though we were
trying," she said. "That's probably the best way, when you're
not trying. It proves that it was really meant to be," I said.
In the weeks that followed, I tried to picture us taking care
of a tiny baby. I could see a featherless, baby bird, squawking
hideously, and me, crawling toward it with an eyedropper, which,
soon, turned into a dagger. Amy was crouched on top of the
couch like a gargoyle, snarling and hissing. That's about as
far as I got trying to imagine us as parents. We didn't tell
anyone our good news. We didn't even talk about it. If Amy
was seeing a doctor, she didn't mention it to me. We were
sailing through some very unreal territory, and the baby was
the captain of our death ship. I watched baseball on TV all
the time, rooting and shouting like a madman, when, in fact,
I had no idea who was playing or what was going on. It was
just to clutter up the empty space in my life that the baby had
created. Amy sat there with me and, occasionally, shouted
something like "Kill those bastards!" Then, she'd glance at
me, almost coquettishly, and smile, hoping I might be a little
proud of her, which I was. She was swelling up with each passing
week. I thought of her belly as a piñata, and, one day, when
I was properly blindfolded, I would beat on it with a stick,
and out would come wonderful candies and fruits and gifts.
Amy should have worn the head of an elephant, and roared loudly
whenever she turned corners in the house. She was that large.
I began to worship her, and, at the same time, fear her. Whenever I brought tea and cookies to her, I bowed, and she

accepted this gesture of obeisance without comment, as though
it were her due. She was the queen, and I, her humble servant.
I took great pride in the performance of my many duties. I did
everything but bathe her. That was an entirely separate operation
jobbed out to independent contractors. I think we both forgot
that a baby had anything to do with any of this. There was so
much to do as it was. I sewed enormous, bejeweled gowns for
the lady. I baked all night. I cooked. I shopped for delicacies.
I chauffeured her to important balls and waited by the side of
the car for hours, counting the stars to keep myself awake.
Not once did I feel sorry for myself, or question my devotion.
And, then, one day she said to me, "Jason, I think it's coming."
"What's coming?" I said. "The baby," she said. My mind went
blank. I literally could not comprehend her words. Our recent
life had been so grand, even though I was a mere servant. "But,
Your Czarina," I said, "there is no room in this house for a baby,
and, besides, I have no time. My time is entirely devoted to
satisfying your needs, which, if you will forgive my saying so,
are many. A baby would break this poor camel's back," I said.
"Be that as it may," she said, "the baby is coming." That night,
I was filled with foreboding. I could hear the pounding hooves
of the wild tribes of Genghis Khan coming over the mountains
to rape and pillage our little kingdom, and I cried for mercy,
but there was none. There was only the little baby from now on.

೮

The Long Journey Home

James Tate

Jeannie had worked as a waitress at the Duck Pond
Cafe for the past eight years, and, during that time, she
had met some pretty strange characters. But, last week,
there was one who beat them all. He was a dead man. He
shuffled in and collapsed in a booth, barely able to hold
his head up. She brought him a glass of water and a menu.
He grasped the glass of water with both hands, and brought
it slowly to his parched lips. Half the water spilled down
his dirty, blue suit, but he didn't seem to mind. "My god,
that's good," he said in a thin, raspy voice. Jeannie poured
him another glass, which he drank immediately. Though his
eyes were almost vacant, he stared at Jeannie's with deep
gratitude. Then he studied the menu excitedly. "I'd like
a double cheeseburger and extra large fries," he said. She
handed the order to Dennis the cook, but said nothing to him
about the deceased customer. She went back and filled his
glass several times, and each time he thanked her and tried
to smile. When his food was finally ready, she delivered it
and he stared at it in awe. "Enjoy," she said, and he replied,
"Yes, yes, I certainly will." She went back to the counter
and watched him devour all of it in several minutes. When
she went to clear his table, he said, "I'd like more of the
same. Is that possible? Are there any rules against that?"
"Certainly not," she said. "Coming right up." She delivered
the order to Dennis, then waited on a family of five who had
just sat down. She was happy that they didn't have a view
of the dead man. After he had finished his second meal, she
asked him if he would care for some dessert. "Oh, yes, indeed,
that would be excellent," he said. He wanted a piece of
apple pie and three scoops of vanilla ice cream. His voice
was coming back to him, and there was even a little gleam in
his eyes. When she delivered his dessert, he thanked her
profusely, and reached out and touched her hand. She started

to freeze, but then caught herself, and grabbed his hand in
hers. "What's your name?" she said. He smiled at her. "Do
you mind if I eat?" he said. "Of course not. That was rude
of me," she said, and walked back to the counter. She delivered
the food to the family of five. They suddenly seemed very loud
and annoying. She much preferred the company of the dead man
who was so quiet and grateful. When he had finished his dessert,
she brought him his check, which he stared at for a long time.
He searched all his pockets to no avail. "That's okay," Jeannie
said. "Don't worry about it." "I was so hungry, I never thought
about the money. That was bad of me," he said. "No, no, it
was an honor to have given you this food. You needed it. I
could see," she said. "But do you have anywhere to go?" His face
looked pained as he thought that over. "Everyone has a place
to go. I'll find one. I don't know how, but, maybe, something
will occur to me. I'll just keep walking. Someone might recognize me,"
he said. "You just needed to get your strength back,"
Jeannie said. He stood up. "I can't thank you enough," he said,
and shook her hand. She stood at the window and watched him walk
down the street, staring into people's faces as they passed.
He was somebody's father or husband or something, but he might
as well be invisible.

ଚ

The Children's Parade. Children who were "suspicious" for having TB either stayed at Bellevue or came each day for treatment. Here, the children are rallying for a park on the grounds of Bellevue so that they could play outdoors, circa 1917. The children are dressed like soldiers, sailors, and Red Cross Nurses, probably as part of the early war effort. Courtesy of Bellevue Hospital Archives: Chest Collection.

The Mask

Sheila Kohler

They asked him to come as soon as possible to discuss a case, a patient who ate things: plastic forks, paper clips, Styrofoam cups, anything he could lay his hands on—apparently he did not discriminate. He had been doing this for years, they said, or so the young psychiatrist understood from the somewhat garbled telephone conversation with a doctor with a heavy Eastern European accent who called from some place upstate.

The psychiatrist telephoned an older colleague for his opinion. The colleague said he had heard of things of this sort, but rarely. He said he was not certain that the diagnosis was the right one.

The psychiatrist took the train. The railroad followed the river for a while, but he did not look up from the article he was writing. He hardly noticed the gray water or the rain falling against the dirty windows. When he did glance up, he saw flat fields spread out on either side. It was late afternoon when he arrived at the small station. The sky was clearing, the light intense. The glare made him shield his eyes. It was very quiet up there with only woods and fields around him. A dog barked in the distance. He stood alone on the platform for a moment, shivering. It was early spring but colder up here. The emptiness of the place, the silence, the evening glare made him feel exposed. He had lived all his life in big cities and thought of the country as a place without culture, the people prejudiced, ignorant and dull; nothing would induce him to live in a place like this, he thought.

The doctor in charge of the hospital, a stout elderly man, with luxuriant white hair and thick glasses, was waiting for the young psychiatrist in the waiting room. With his striped tie blown over his shoulder, the doctor hurried toward the psychiatrist as he came in the door. The elderly doctor seemed flustered, dropped some papers on the floor, could hardly bring himself to shake the psychiatrist's hand. He said, "So good of you to come all this way," and inclined his head deferentially.

They drove along a rutted road in the doctor's battered car. The road narrowed, dipped a little. They crossed a small bridge that needed a coat of paint. The doctor pointed out the institution through the car's window as they approached. In the distance, rising up through the trees, the psychiatrist saw the building. It had been a grand hotel or a mansion at one time, the doctor told the psychiatrist proudly. It was a nineteenth century edifice in a state of disrepair, with a sort of porch with Greek columns, the white paint flaking, and woods on either side.

The doctor ushered the psychiatrist down a long green corridor into a conference room. A bare yellow bulb hung from the ceiling over a table covered with green baize. The varnished floor glistened. For a moment the psychiatrist thought of Van Gogh. He had had a passion for paintings as a boy, but had given up his studies of art to become a psychiatrist.

Several faces were lifted toward him. Introductions were made. There was a psychologist, a thin woman no longer young, with a string of bright green beads around her scrawny neck; a doctor who came from the Philippines; some Indian residents; an Irish intern. The psychologist immediately embarked on a long history of the patient in an unexpectedly deep voice, twisting her green beads around her fingers nervously as she told the psychiatrist what seemed to him trivial and tiresome details about the patient's life, about the patient's mother, his violent father who had shot the patient's girlfriend's father and was now in jail. From her remarks the psychiatrist learned only that the patient had been hospitalized for most of his life; several experts had been consulted; he had received various treatments, none of which had had any effect, and the previous week he had once again eaten a plastic fork, had been operated on, had almost died.

"The condition seems to be chronic," the psychologist said and twisted her green beads tightly around her neck.

The doctor in charge sighed, adjusted his glasses and said, "Everything possible has been done for the poor man, but nothing makes any difference."

The young psychiatrist felt bored and hungry. He remembered he had not had time for lunch. He asked if it would be possible to have a cup of tea. Someone brought him one, which he drank fast, slopping the tea into the saucer. He wished someone would offer him something to eat. A vision of a large bowl of popcorn rose up in his mind.

He became aware that the psychologist was saying, "After he's worn it for a while the behavior stops, temporarily, at least." The psychiatrist thought of something. "Did someone say the man suffers from asthma?" the psychiatrist asked suddenly. They all nodded cheerfully. The psychiatrist nodded back, looked around at the faces, noticed the Philippine doctor smiling at him genially. Someone else, one of the Indian residents, perhaps, said, "It has proved most effective, when the man can be brought to wear it."

It was then that he caught, out of the side of his eye, the sight of something dark on the table. For a moment he thought of a small child wearing the thing so as not to hurt his head when it was banged against a wall. He asked if he could see it. Someone passed it to him. He held it in his hands, turned it around. There were two slits for the eyes and a small opening for the nose and tiny perforations where it covered the cheeks as if to allow the beard to grow through.

The psychiatrist asked to see the patient. The doctor in charge suggested one of the male nurses remain in the room. The psychiatrist said, "I don't think that will be necessary," but thought of the patient he had once treated— a rich Arab— who had taken a bite out of his cheek. He said, "Well, let him stand behind the door."

A male nurse brought the patient into the room. The nurse left the room, locked the door from the outside but remained looking through the glass panel at the top of the door.

The psychiatrist introduced himself, shook the patient's hand, a large red hand. The patient grasped his hand firmly and asked, "Dr. Wren? Don't I know you from somewhere?"

The psychiatrist smiled and shook his head, though for a second he did think there was something familiar about the patient. He was a tall, loose-limbed, ugly fellow with reddish hair and a small scar on his upper lip.

They sat down facing one another across the wide table. The psychiatrist asked the patient about his life in this place. The patient leaned toward the psychiatrist and looked at him with intelligent dark brown eyes. He looked as though he wanted to tell the psychiatrist—and him alone—something important, but he said nothing. After a while, the psychiatrist asked, "How do you feel?" The patient said suddenly, "You have to do something for me!" The psychiatrist nodded, smiled. "I will try." He gave the patient a piece of paper and a pencil and asked the man to draw the face of a clock and set the hands pointing to ten minutes to three.

The patient asked, "Why are your hands shaking?" The psychiatrist stretched forth his large long-fingered hands and looked at them. He laughed. "Too much caffeine."

The patient drew all the numbers of the clock bunched up into one quadrant, the wrong one. The psychiatrist looked at the drawing carefully and then at the patient's face for a moment. "Try it again," the psychiatrist urged, but the patient drew the same thing. Then the psychiatrist frowned and took out his address book, a paper clip, a pen, and a piece of paper from his pocket and placed them on the edge of the table before him. He told the patient to look at the objects and to try to remember them.

The patient reached out suddenly for the paper clip, but the psychiatrist caught his hand in time, shook his head. "Just look," he said, and turned his head slightly to one side and smiled.

The patient said, "I promise I'll never do anything like that again," and turned and looked over his shoulder toward the window where the male nurse stood watching. The psychiatrist urged the patient to study the objects in order to remember them. The patient stared at the objects for a moment. Then the psychiatrist slipped the objects into his pocket. He asked the patient if he could name them. The patient shook his head impatiently and leaned closer to the psychiatrist and whispered, "All I want is to leave this place. Can you imagine what it's like in a place like this, being watched all the time?" Again he glanced at the nurse.

The psychiatrist asked the patient if he was sure he could not remember the objects shown to him, but the patient only rose from his chair and walked over to a window. He stood with his back to the young psychiatrist, looking out the window, his large red hands lifted to either side of his head and pressed against the pane of glass. The psychiatrist, too, rose and looked out another window, at the rain that had begun to fall again. He noticed the thick silver drops falling obliquely, caught in the lamplight like ash. All around the place were open fields. It was farming country now, though once, the psychiatrist thought, there had probably been elegant estates along the river.

The psychiatrist thought of something else. There was something he wanted to know, he said, a question he wanted to ask. Haltingly, he asked the man if he was drawn to some things more than others. The man turned slowly and seemed to be considering the psychiatrist. He had the impression that the man was about to speak frankly to him. Then he walked toward the psychiatrist and stood beside him, with something like collusion in his eyes. The man smiled slightly as he said, "I try to find things that fit my personality."

The psychiatrist shuddered and felt his heart begin to flutter irregularly.

The man moved closer to the psychiatrist, standing right beside him, so that the psychiatrist realized the patient was about the same height as he was. The patient came even closer and whispered in his ear, "They watch me, or they make me wear the mask." The psychiatrist stared at the man and noticed a despairing and agitated expression in his eyes. The man glanced over his shoulder and jerked his head toward the male nurse. The psychiatrist waved the nurse away from the window. The nurse hesitated, raised his eyebrows inquiringly. The psychiatrist made an impatient gesture, and the nurse stepped away from the window. The psychiatrist could hear him talking to someone in the corridor in Spanish. The staccato Spanish words, which the psychiatrist did not understand, sounded loud and angry.

The psychiatrist sat down and gestured to the patient to do the same. He leaned toward the man and said in a low voice, "I think I may be able to help you." The man's eyes turned bright. The psychiatrist asked if anyone had given him these tests before. The man said, "Tests?"

The psychiatrist raised his eyebrows and shook his head. He said, "It is possible you may be able to leave this place."

"When?" the man asked, staring at the psychiatrist, his eyes glittering. The man began walking back and forth across the small room restlessly, as though hunting for something. The psychiatrist could hear the sound of the patient's shoes squeaking on the linoleum floor as he shifted direction. Outside the window the rain, the psychiatrist became aware, had stopped. The sky was very black, starless. "Further tests will have to be made, but it is possible that there is something wrong with your brain that could be cured by surgery; I will speak to the people in charge here."

The man stood still and said, "They will never let me leave, particularly not if there has been some mistake."

"It won't be right away, and it will be tricky, but I promise you I will see you get the necessary tests." The psychiatrist looked at his watch. He added, "I'm afraid it is very late now. I have to catch the last train in half an hour." He stood up and put on his coat and gloves.

The man moved with such sudden speed and in such an unforeseen manner that the psychiatrist was unable to react. The man had his hands on the collar of the psychiatrist's coat. The man said, "I'm certain we have met somewhere before."

The psychiatrist wanted to tell the man that patients often told him that; that he had patients waiting for him in the city; that if he missed his train he would have to spend the night up here in a stranger's house; that he hated the country. But he looked into the man's face and saw the hope in his eyes, and then he sat down again and took off his leather gloves.

The doctor drove them back to his house. It was surrounded by trees, and all the lights were lit. When they walked into the hall the psychiatrist could smell something cooking. Though he had eaten almost nothing all day, the strong odor made him feel slightly sick. He was ushered into a stuffy, cluttered living room and was left alone. He walked uncomfortably across the thick carpet, looking at the pathetic signs of cheap luxury strewn around the room: the gilt candelabra, the brocade slipcovers, the tasseled poufs. It was very warm in the room, and through the thin walls the psychiatrist could hear much anxious muttering and the clattering of dishes. He heard something fall to the floor and a little shriek followed by what sounded like a slap.

Suddenly a strange thin sound struck up; a monotonous, whining voice was singing a sad song. The music rose and fell endlessly and evoked strange, unpleasant echoes in the psychiatrist's mind. For a moment he felt slightly giddy, and then his heart started to beat irregularly. He collapsed on the sofa, bent over. He even put his hands over his mouth.

When he looked up, he realized he was being watched. A slim young woman in a bright pink dress which looked too big for her, was standing shyly by the door. She wore gold sandals and her long black hair loose. It glowed, glossy as a blackbird. There was a flower in her hair. She smiled and then walked toward him, swinging her hips gracefully, holding her head high, a tray poised in one hand. She placed the tray carefully on the table. The psychiatrist stood up, introduced himself, reached out to shake her hand. She touched his hand briefly, her small hand very cold in his. She introduced herself solemnly as the doctor's youngest daughter. She poured something carefully from the pitcher on the tray into a small glass and handed him the glass and a napkin. All the while he was sipping the sweet liqueur and wiping his mouth, she watched him intently. It seemed to the psychiatrist that the girl had the same hopeful stare in her eyes as the patient in the institution.

The dinner table was arrayed with a vast number of dishes in heavy sauces, though only two places were laid. There were flowers floating in a gilt bowl of water in the center, and the yellow candlesticks were lit. The elderly doctor and the young psychiatrist dined alone, sitting opposite one another at one end of the table. The psychiatrist asked if the doctor's wife would not join them. The elderly doctor looked down at the table and said his wife had not recovered completely after an illness. She was troubled by chronic arthritis.

The psychiatrist asked how many children the doctor had. The doctor smiled and said God had been good to him; he had six, and several grandchildren, as well, though, of course, the burden of providing for such a large family fell on his shoulders most heavily at times, and he looked at the psychiatrist and added that he was sure he would understand.

The psychiatrist said that indeed, he did, that he himself had two small boys and that was quite heavy enough for him. Then the doctor clicked his fingers and the daughter who had served the drinks came in with a plate of warm, buttered bread covered with a linen napkin. She served the psychiatrist with the same hopeful gaze. He said he was sorry not to make the wife's acquaintance, and that the doctor had a very lovely daughter. The doctor smiled, turned towards the girl and spread his fingers gently over her shoulder and said that to him all his daughters were lovely.

The doctor drank several glasses of wine and urged the psychiatrist to drink and eat. He said that wine gave him a headache and that he was not very hungry. The bread was heavy and tasteless, and the dishes so heavily spiced they brought tears to his eyes. He asked for an aspirin and explained that he had trouble with his heart from time to time—arrhythmia, he said. The elderly doctor clicked his tongue and told him to watch out for stroke.

The singing in the background was softer now but continued monotonously. The room grew hotter. The psychiatrist loosened his tie, asked if the doctor would mind if he removed his jacket. He was sweating and feeling increasingly unwell. At first he could not concentrate at all on what the doctor was saying, waiting only for the man to stop speaking in order to broach the subject of the patient, but after a while he found himself listening as the doctor went on rapidly and at length about the institution.

There was something almost incantatory about the doctor's accented words with their singsong cadence, their old-fashioned formality. The doctor said that on the whole he could say without lying that the patients were really quite contented in that place. Of course, one could not hope to cure them— how could one hope to cure such ill people? God's will would be done, what was bound to be could not be otherwise—but in his humble opinion many of the patients seemed much improved. They even put on plays themselves from time to time; the eminent psychiatrist should really try to find time in his busy schedule to assist. The spectacle was really most edifying and there were many diverse workshops to keep the patients busy: basket weaving, music therapy, art therapy. There was even a rather large indoor swimming pool for them. The swimming seemed, in his modest opinion, to be most helpful, the doctor said. Occasionally some of the patients were even given the opportunity to go horseback riding on a nearby farm. If only the eminent psychiatrist could see their glowing faces when they came back from a ride! What a gratifying sight! Truly, many of them had grown very much attached to the people in charge who, though they did not always have the highest qualifications—unfortunately it was not always possible to get people with the highest qualifications to come up to a place like this and work with patients this ill—were very sensitive to the patients' needs. Everyone, the doctor said, as he looked at the psychiatrist anxiously, was doing his very best.

The psychiatrist interrupted, said he was certain they were doing their best. Then he attempted to speak of the patient he had seen that afternoon, but his head was spinning and his heartbeat irregular, and he had felt obliged to drink some of the sweet wine, which made him feel nauseated.

He suggested that certain tests should be done to determine whether the origin of the patient's behavior might be organic. "Organic!" the elderly doctor exclaimed and clasped his fine hands together dramatically. The psychiatrist asked if there was any good reason why routine tests of this sort had never been done. The doctor said he was sure such tests were not necessary, that in his opinion if such a thing were discovered, which seemed extremely doubtful —after all, the diagnosis of mental illness had been made many years ago, long before the doctor had arrived in that place—the patient would not be in a condition to undergo surgery, would in any event be unwilling, if one could speak of his having a will at all, to go through anything as traumatic as surgery, but naturally he, as the doctor in charge of the mental institution, would follow the eminent psychiatrist's suggestion, and with a trembling hand, he passed the dish of stewed chicken which lay swimming in its oily sauce.

The psychiatrist declined, said he was feeling very tired. The doctor went on talking about the hospital, giving the psychiatrist all sorts of details and using many learned terms.

The room the psychiatrist was to occupy for the night was very small and airless. He did not undress fully but lay in his shirt and socks, tossing back and forth. His head continued to ache and he felt unwell. His heart beat irregularly. He heard strange rustlings and murmuring from the room next door. He could see a light under the door. He had the impression he was being watched. Finally, toward morning, he put his coat back on, staggered down the stairs and went outside into the cool air.

A faint beam of light pierced the clouds, and the psychiatrist could make out the mental institution in the distance: it glimmered white as a ghost in the early mist. He thought of the man shut up in there, year after year, without any reason, his movements constantly watched, his breathing stifled by the mask. He heard the patient's words: "All I want is to leave this place." As he looked up into the branches of a slim birch tree in the muted light of day, a memory came to him.

Standing in the faint first light, his heart beating irregularly, the sweat trickling down his forehead, his vision dim, he seemed to see his own father's tall figure, caught in a beam of light from the open door, standing darkly in the hall. It was the day his father left their house for the war, never to come back. The psychiatrist saw his mother's face as she bent over him, watching him with that anxious light in her dark eyes. He smelled the panic on her breath as she drew her face closer and closer to his and held him ever more tightly in her arms until his ribs ached. She was whispering words to him, words he was never to forget. She was saying that he would have to take care of her now, that he would have to be her good, good boy, that he would have to be her little man.

In that instant the psychiatrist realized what it had all been leading toward—the spotlessness of his clothes, the orderliness of his room, the smoothness of his bed, the boat he had carved in wood, the hands kept outside the blanket all through the long night, the piles of clean dishes, the cleaned oven, the shoveled snow, the repaired lamps, the endless studies, the excellent grades, the prescribed medication, the brilliant interpretations, the published articles, the endless hours of listening and listening. He thought of the art studies he had abandoned, the long hours he had spent in the museums looking at paintings he had loved, and he remembered one fall afternoon in Paris on his junior year abroad when he had sat outside in a cafe near the Seine and felt the sun on his shoulders and sipped a delicious strong, dark espresso with a little sliver of lemon peel. He thought of a line from a poem that he had never really understood: "Else a great prince in a prison lies," and the meaning became clear to him. In one instant he realized where it was all taking him, what it all meant.

As he was thinking this he heard the same sound he had heard the night before, the same strange whining sound, the sad voice singing its ancient and incomprehensible song. It shattered the silence of the early morning. It seemed to him that it was this music that made him feel so unwell and would have that effect again.

He hurried back inside and picked up his watch from beside the bed. He walked down the corridor and knocked loudly on the bedroom door. The doctor emerged almost immediately and fully dressed, as though he had been waiting for the psychiatrist's knock. He asked the doctor to drive him to the station in order to catch the early morning train. The doctor did not offer him breakfast but told him to wait in the hall.

The psychiatrist could hear the sound of the car's wheels spinning on the stones of the driveway. The doctor drove the car to the front door and jumped out with alacrity to usher the psychiatrist into the front seat. He drove the psychiatrist fast and in silence to the station, as though he were afraid the psychiatrist might change his mind on the way. The elderly doctor shook the psychiatrist's hand warmly as he thanked him for his hospitality, and almost pushed the psychiatrist up the train steps. The doctor stood grinning and waving enthusiastically as the train drew out of the station. ৪১

Why

Sharon Dolin

> *in memory of Judith Levey Kurlander*

and the answer is silence amid such gold-silver electrum
(as Correggio used to paint the heavens).
Why are so many Job-challenged
as Judith—not as so many saw her
nor as Artemisia knew her (she who slew
before being slain)—not *her* Judith but *my* Judith
Amazon-carved by cancer and by delight
in the things of the world—why is she—
after ten years—stricken again
so that now her womb—three times home—
is removed—and maybe her life? Is evil prospering
worse than the good hit by blight?
I don't think so—or know what to make of this whirlwind—
or why the Leviathan still gets to lash
his spiked tail and strike down or why
the all-powerful has chosen to withdraw and
recede like some deuced cardplayer who
refuses to show his hand.

৪৩

Home treatment of TB: taking the cure in winter, circa 1909. Courtesy of Bellevue Hospital Archives: Chest Collection.

Mood Swings

Erica Funkhouser

When criticized, she craves butter.
When praised, salt.
Sadness calls for inadequate outerwear.
Exhilaration for ultra violet.
All feelings are unhealthy.
For solitude, driving too fast.
For lack of solitude, Scotch.
Money, success and attention cure everything.
Money, success and attention make no difference at all.
Open the window on trouble.
Close the window on luck.
Baseball statistics to ease boredom.
The botanical names of plants to prevent vanity.
If uncertain, dive into freezing water.
If empty, climb clouds.
There's nothing she hasn't tried.
Lacking speech, she pierced her tongue.
Lacking sleep, she invited stones into her body.
A precipice when enamored.
A coil when confident.
Some days one mood is enough to chase away another:
stubbornness beats back fury beats gratified beats silly.
She has used pitiful to subdue commanding
and austere to embarrass sweet.
Two moods of equal experience
will stare each other down until one blinks.
She has heard pride sniffling in its sleeve
and willingness cursing its place at the table.
Others are always arriving, in and out,
like a bat, like a bandit, like a break in the current.
Change to remedy poison. Poison to remedy thirst.
Thirst to remedy simplification. Poor simplification—
that one never survives its own arrival.

Rubbing My Mother's Back

Erica Funkhouser

She remembers me as restless
and impulsive, legs wrapped
around a gallop
or swimming until no one
could spot me,

so she is surprised when my fingers
with their large knuckles
stroll the miserable ridge
of her backbone
and turn up comfort.
Not a snap but a bend.

She was never one to imagine
our secret destinations.
She let us stay away for hours
without worry.
In exchange for our privacy,
we brought her violets
or the skull of a fox.

Now her dry spine takes her
where it will,
reckless with age,
and she imagines the worst.

This, too, a mother:
cooing and sighing,
little gasps of horror and relief
as my hands let her know
where I am, where I am going.

ॐ

Imminence

H. L. McNaugher

In the bath you're alone to think about the news. You decide the way to proceed is to mummy up your voice and heart and observe shrewdly for the next decade or so. This way, nothing will surprise you. The rising scald of the water makes you sweaty and lightheaded. Lying back, eyelids slumping, you imagine arriving at your mother's in Cleveland, a city you could certainly get used to, explore by bike, pausing only to assess the horizon of low, broad buildings, while fine-tuning your total disengagement over cups of coffee on windy corners. Your mother, a chaplain, arrived in this town only last year and she is now, you've been informed, a patient herself. Again. In your daydream you're there to see to her. You stay in the one-bedroom apartment she'd been so excited to get just this past August. You imagine spending every November night on the sofa bed she purchased in place of a second bedroom for you. The lean wood floors stretch toward a view of Lake Erie and downtown. Six flights below is Shaker Square, all Hungarian food, antique and coffee shops crammed with the stuff of community. You forsake all this to cuddle up to the radio, the bookcase, the kitchen and the bath of a single woman with a new life in a strange, flat city—your mother.

Your mother hosts someone else's kidney inside her body. Before it was hers, it belonged to her younger sister, your Aunt Sandra. The kidney is now fifty-years-old, born and bred in Sandy until it was forty. The life of a transplanted kidney can range from mere hopefulness, those first few teetering seconds, to twenty years, with its chances of adjusting to a new but familiar landscape always rosier when the donor is a living relative versus an unrelated, impassive cadaver. Last April you traveled from Pittsburgh to Cleveland to celebrate your mother's ten-year anniversary with her sister's little bean. Aunt Sandy was there too, of course, and in the gawky moments of gratitude you tried gazing her way, her own stare boring damningly back through you and into your lifestyle—the closely-cropped hair, the cocksure gait in mannish trousers. Normally not one to blink first, you spent the rest of that afternoon gathering your posture, keeping your hands out of your pockets. Sandy is a fundamentalist Christian from central Florida, you remind yourself now, months later, nude and uninhibited in the tub. Her beliefs dictate that she donate kidneys to the needy, and that her green-eyed scrutiny remain righteous and serene, while nails fly out to crucify the lesbian likes of her sister's daughter.

Smack in the middle of your twenties, you are, naturally, waiting for your life to change without much input from your own will. You lift your young biker legs up out of the bath water. Ever fretting over things like circulation, varicose veins, you stretch calves and quads straight up in the air, ten toes winking at you through the steam. To achieve optimum agony, you try envisioning your feet flat against the ceiling the way a former Tae Kwon Do instructor commanded. Instead you end up watching the water channel through matted shin hair to lag in the scars at your knees. You shut your eyes to greet a sick mom in need, a bed that disappears each morning, a dumb job doing little but with grace, and a small smile for neighbors you don't know. And for only the four-hundred-and-ninth time today you contemplate changing, if not the whole crummy world, then at least your own, and that opportunity lives—and is perhaps dying—in Cleveland.

It is not lost on you that you might be the next donor. You're over 18 now, but still healthy, strong, resilient. Two shapely oxblood blessings, only one of which you need, lay waiting in your back. You think about being 15 again, under age even to give blood—useless and sullen at the bedside of a frail, sallow woman you were sure wouldn't make it. These days you wonder what the potentially empty space behind your abdomen would do to your mountain biking. Your back constricts at the thought of tree roots and cobblestones jostling what was once packed tight, but is now a soup of unattached sinew whose arterial routes lead suddenly nowhere.

You can't remember how long your mother was on dialysis. It wasn't for more than a year, yet interminable, and you will never have her there again in the unlikely event that any of this is left up to you. The sprawling orange art deco building; the last stop in Oakland, shadowy neighborhood to Pittsburgh's finest hospitals. Once a week guilt overrode feigned adolescent indifference; you donned an equally feigned graciousness to show up at the clinic and ride home with her on the bus. In your bright blue seat you distracted yourself with a clammy, gripping fear for both your lives—every passenger was a rapist or thief, every thinning gasp of daylight, homicidal. Your mother went to dialysis three times a week. Doctors had implanted a loop in the inside of her arm above her wrist—a graft, they called it. You could see its raised racetrack through her flimsy skin, and the single clotted-up bruise of a hole where the needle lay stuck for hours each session, sucking out the sullied blood and pushing the laundered stuff back in. In the decade between reality and recollection, everything about the dialysis center becomes orange—the building sign, the walls, even the machines themselves, clunky as cafeteria furniture or the first computer.

The graft has all but disintegrated in the ten years of disuse—abandonment in this instance being a blessing. Your head submerged and releasing bubbles, you think of all such tiny miracles that have contained the metastasizing misfortune of your mother's life: that she chose Pittsburgh, transplant capital of the world, in which to nearly die of renal failure; that her sister hears God talking and was listening that day in 1988; that her inner arm could harbor a graft at all, that it didn't get sewn into her pitiful sunken chest.

Standing up to drip-dry, you look down your long face to survey big breasts and invincible hips. Your legs go forever and without your glasses on, your mighty feet blur under water. This is your father's body you're living in. It occurs to you that your considerable kidney may not even fit inside the dainty nook that is your mother. You recall how they leave the bad kidneys in there, surgically shoved aside to atrophy. Your mother could soon have three totally functionless organs shriveling inside her.

You're careful not to mention any of this to her over the phone. Out of the bath, sitting on your futon in boxers and an old swim team tee shirt, you yearn to be called to her side, but fail to offer yourself. She's simultaneously discouraged and grateful for ten good years that may or may not be ending any day now. "They just can't say yet." She tells you how all last week she couldn't get her stockings past her thighs, bloated with a backlog of toxins and fluid. You realize, in the clear, remorseful hush that comes with hindsight, that she has sounded more and more fatigued over the past month, and that each conversation ended before anyone suggested it was, alas, over. You try and remember a day in your life when your mother wasn't flattened by exhaustion.

Your mother, the chaplain, deals with the dying and deserted every single day, and her threshold for the emotional havoc of strangers has stretched boundlessly homeward all your life. Growing up, quality time with Mom meant evenings with "Trapper John, M.D." and "St. Elsewhere," which you'd watch together from the cornflower-blue corduroy sofa, your mother anxious as a Pirates' fan, rating out loud the lingo and suspense based on her own day's drama. She still doesn't ask you about your days, or listen when you ramble like a wife about them anyway. You've given up confronting her on this one—"Mom, you're not listening to me." She defends her right to ignore you, calling "burn-out...distraction," your maddening martyr of a mom, who can't watch an infomercial about a simple laser procedure without offering bereavement counseling to the actors on the screen. You love her to death and know you will scarcely be able to bear the intimacy of what's about to come. ❧

The Liver Nephew

Susan Ito

Parker Katami had just come back from a four-mile run when he opened his mail—a photocopied article from the *New England Journal of Medicine* tucked into an envelope. He pulled it out with hot, damp hands. There were a few lines, in his uncle's trembling, miniscule print, scribbled in the margin. *Dear Nephew,* it said, *I must ask you for a rather large favor.* The article was about a groundbreaking medical procedure called Living Donor Transplant. The favor, it turned out, was for Parker to donate half of his liver to Uncle Min.

Parker leaned against his front door for several minutes, panting and staring at the brass mail slot through which the envelope had been spat. Thin rivulets of sweat streaked down his neck and forked around his clavicle like transparent veins. He put his hand to his stomach, and then around toward his ribs, patting the skin. He wasn't even quite sure where his liver was located.

Contact with his uncle had been infrequent recently—not much beyond the chipper, generic holiday cards that his Auntie Reiko sent out every year, signed with both their names—but Parker's childhood memories of Uncle Min were tinged with comfort. Parker seemed to remember some mention of Uncle's being ill, but this was to be expected with people of their age, wasn't it? His own parents were both dead, his father of a brain tumor some years ago, his mother from emphysema. Did his uncle really expect to trick Nature, and gain new life from having a younger person's liver? It sounded hopeful and naïve, like cryogenics. Parker squinted at the medical article again, clotted with words he didn't understand, and then tossed it onto the coffee table.

He didn't like the idea of going to a hospital, much less letting them open up his body and take something out. He had seen enough of hospitals with his parents: his father's wrists tied to the metal bedrails with cotton gauze rope, his mother straining to pull in air through bluish lips.

He went into the kitchen and snapped the metal ring from a can of ginger ale, took a long noisy gulp. After rummaging through a junk drawer for a ballpoint pen, he studied the article and then slapped it face down on the table. *Uncle M,* he printed on the back of the page, *wish I could help but I can't. Sorry.* As he contemplated whether or not to write "Love," before signing his name, the phone rang.

"Hello."

"Paka-chan!" The high, breathy voice of Auntie Reiko, who always sounded on the edge of hysterical giggles.

"Hi, Auntie." He scribbled a little star shape on the paper, and then wrote *Love, Parker.*

"Parker, tell me, did you get Uncle's letter? It should be there by now." A rumbling voice in the background, Uncle Min saying something. Muffle muffle, and then a hard click as her wedding ring hit the receiver.

"Auntie? Yeah, it came today."

"Oh, Parker..." Her voice rose even higher, tightening and shrinking, until it squeezed into the corner between the ceiling and walls. "Your uncle is so sick, he's suffering so, *kawai soh*, poor thing."

"I'm sorry. I didn't realize." He chewed a bit of skin away from his thumbnail, and closed his eyes. Uncle suffering? He didn't want to know.

She sniffled loudly. "So you'll help him, *neh?* Your papa's *o toto?*"

"What about Patty and George, Auntie?" His cousins.

"Oh, Parker, they couldn't. So you the last hope. Doctor says he can't last long like this, maybe two months. Parker-chan, please!" Her voice was broken and wet.

"Auntie, I don't know, my job..." Perhaps this was something they could understand, his career. He had recently been promoted to editor of a slick but faltering Denver-area magazine, targeted toward urban athletes.

She was now weeping uncontrollably.

Parker's blood thumped so loudly in his ears that he could barely hear her voice. Uncle Min was talking in the background beyond her sobs, and he sounded just like Parker's father, the way Parker remembered his voice from long ago. He looked out the window, at a woman on the sidewalk in a red raincoat. A black dog was pulling away from her, nosing at a paper cup in the gutter. "Let me talk to him," he said.

He paced in his apartment for two days before he gave way to his desperate confusion and dialed Joel's number. They had agreed there would be no phone calls, but this constituted an emergency, didn't it?

Joel picked up on the first ring. There was jazz playing in the background, and more than one person talking.

"Joel. It's me."

There was a pause, and then, "Hey. Hey, what's up?" A strained kind of casual.

"Listen, Joel, sorry to call so late, but something really freaky is happening and..."

"Wait a sec, let me go in the other room." The sound of a door closing, and the music abruptly stopped. "What? You're not sick, are you?"

"No, it isn't me. It's my uncle."

"Your uncle? What uncle?" Parker realized that he'd never mentioned his remaining family to Joel, nor Joel to them.

"My dad's brother. Min. Well, he's got some medical problem, something serious, and they're asking me to donate my liver."

"What? You mean if you get in a car wreck?"

"No, Joel, that's the thing. They want me to donate half of it, *now*. They call it a living transplant."

Parker heard water running, and the squeaky sound of the medicine cabinet door. He hadn't been in Joel's apartment in a month, and suddenly he was sick with longing. "Joel? You still there?"

"Wait. He wants *half* of your *liver?*" Parker gripped the phone hopefully. Maybe Joel was understanding how important this was, how impossible it was to make this decision alone.

"Yeah. It's this new thing, this experimental..." Parker was rushing his words into the phone.

"And what are you supposed to do with just half a liver?"

"Supposedly it grows back." It sounded insane now, telling it to Joel.

"Huh. That's... interesting." The sound of running water.

"So what do you think? Do you think I should do it?" Parker ached to say, *Please come with me*, but he couldn't.

"I don't know what to tell you, Park. Listen, man..." The bathroom door swung open, and the receiver filled with partying sounds again. "Hey, it's your decision."

"But I'm asking *you*. Do you think you could come over? Maybe later?"

"I'm sorry, Park. I've got people here." The voices and the music began mixing with Joel's voice, growing louder—he was probably walking into the kitchen now—and Parker knew that his five minutes of privacy was up, that he was being firmly led to the door.

"Yeah, I know," he said in a low voice, and hung up.

And so Parker didn't say no, but he didn't say yes. He had conversations with his uncle's physicians, both the primary-care doctor and the hotshot guy in charge of the transplant team, who spoke rapidly and repeated himself, a verbal twitching. The only clear thing that Parker recalled from the conversation was the number two: two percent mortality rate among living donors. He repeated that to the doctor to make sure he understood. "Mortality rate: that means dead, right?"

"Right, right."

"And you don't think I'm too… old for this? I'm thirty-eight, almost." His birthday less than a month away.

"No, not at all. It's a good age, a good, good age."

Parker thought of a morning when he was seven or eight, bouncing on the edge of his father's bed. *It's my birthday, Papa. Say Happy Birthday.* He bounced and chanted until his father rose up from his pillow and smacked him above the ear. *Here's something for your birthday!*

There was one present he remembered vividly: a kite that Uncle Min had brought him for his birthday, a tiger on red silk. Uncle had taken him and Patty and George to a park in Berkeley, a lonely place that was empty of trees, just grassy hills with a wind that tore at their clothes and set the tiger pouncing against the sky.

He agreed to the blood test, and when it came up a match, he packed his suitcase. A thick envelope arrived in the mail from his aunt and uncle, containing a first-class airplane ticket to San Francisco. He had never flown first class in his life. *I'm the fatted calf,* he thought, *being led to slaughter.* He notified his publisher that he'd be out of town, saying that the associate editor would handle things while he was gone. He wrote a note to Joel and left it prominently on the coffee table, in case Joel should happen to stop by. He still had Parker's key.

He boarded the airplane ahead of everyone else, along with the wealthy, the infirm, and the parents traveling with small children. When the flight attendant led him to the wide leather seat, his eyes darted about momentarily, as if he was going to be thrown out. Parker sat down gingerly. How inexpressibly more comfortable the first-class seat was, how delicious the food, how reassuring the heavy thick silverware, the actual china plates. They brought him ice water in a glass goblet, and a steaming towel to press against his face. He tried not to think of the Last Supper.

Uncle Min opened the front door as soon as the taxi pulled up to the curb. "Take a cab, not the shuttle van," they had told him. The house, outer Sunset district, was the same as he remembered—pale pink, unremarkable in the rows and rows of minty little houses all lined up together. Parker remembered wishing, when he was small, that he could lick them, thinking they would taste like the candies next to the cash register at the Ocean Diner.

Uncle Min was wearing his bathrobe and slippers, even though it was four in the afternoon. His skin was a frightening amber color, and his eyes golden, like a cat's. They glossed over with tears as he took Parker's hands in both of his. Auntie Reiko was right behind him, shaking her head with emotion, her hand covering her mouth. Parker reached past his uncle to embrace her, her dyed-black hair smelling like onions and Pond's lotion.

"Dinner ready soon," she said. "You go, go, lie down and rest. Bring your suitcase to George's room. And wash your hands, those planes are so *kitanai.*"

"I don't need to rest, Auntie," Parker said. "It wasn't that long a flight." He carried his bag up the half-flight of steps to his cousin's room. The room had been preserved as a kind of shrine to George's boyhood: posters of punk bands, the electric bass on its stand, the rows and rows of sci-fi novels on the shelf. Nothing had been tampered with since George, the prized son, had graduated from high school. Parker's own childhood home didn't even exist anymore; the year he'd gone to college, his parents had moved into a small townhouse in another state.

When Parker returned to the living room, Uncle Min shuffled past him and collapsed in the red easy chair in the living room. It had dishtowels on either arm to cover up the bald spots. "Come on, sit down then. You want a beer? Reiko, get him a beer."

Parker sat on the piano bench, half covered in unopened mail and catalogs. The television was tuned to a tennis match. A gray band of dialogue scrolled up the screen. AND IT'S LOVE NOTHING.

"How come the volume's off?" Parker asked.

"Ah, those announcers, their voices give me a headache." Uncle Min waved his hand disgustedly at the screen. The stereo was on, a scratchy LP of "Man of La Mancha." Parker and Uncle Min sat and watched the yellow ball silently plunking back and forth. *To dream the impossible dream.* By the time Aunt Reiko brought a tray with a bottle of beer and a bowl of rice crackers, Uncle Min was slumped in the chair, snoring.

Parker watched the soundless game until his eyes came to rest on the lacquer box on top of the television set: his uncle's Go game. He lifted it down, and a rush of remembered anticipation filled his throat as he opened it: the same smooth black and white pebbles he'd played with when he was small, their cool weight, the clicking sound they made in his palm. He laid them out on the wooden board, rows of ten. Parker had never actually learned how to play; he just loved making patterns of the smooth stone on wood. He counted out ninety-eight of the blacks. They nearly filled the board, solid, dark. Then he plucked two white from the box and considered their small stark forms against the black field. That was two percent.

"Parker! Baby cousin!" His cousin Patty arrived just as the tennis match was finishing. Her Minnie Mouse voice was a younger version of her mother's. She was only a year and a half older than he, and it annoyed him that she still called him Baby.

Parker awkwardly draped his arm around her. "Hi, Patty."

"Look at you!" She squeezed his upper arm. "You're in such good shape, Parker. Are you still running?"

Patty was twenty pounds heavier than he remembered, and her bangs and round black haircut made her cheeks even plumper. He wondered if she remembered kissing him under the ping-pong table one teenaged Thanksgiving, her mouth tasting like cherry lifesavers, his hands clutching the black rope of her hair. It was so long it had brushed the floor. She was the only girl he had ever kissed.

Brad, Patty's *hakujin* husband, gave him a high-five. "How you doing, man." Brad was the kind of guy who bounced on the balls of his feet, who wore athletic shoes all the time, and who would want to play touch football on the lawn after dinner. Their two year old *hapa* kid wouldn't look at him when Brad held him up. "Say hello to Uncle Parker."

"I'm not his uncle," said Parker; he didn't like joining Brad in false joviality. "We're first cousins once-removed." He reached out to tickle the boy under the chin, but it turned into more of a poke. The boy treaded air and started to cry.

Aunt Reiko came into the living room and held up her hands, red and chapped, as if she had just finished building a snowman without mittens on. Parker wondered if she had the kind of illness that makes a person scrub their hands every five minutes.

"*Itadakimasu*," she called out cheerily. "Please come eat. Everyone wash hands first."

"What about George?" Parker said.

Everyone's face suddenly fell flat, and Parker looked out the window. A teenager from the pale yellow house across the street was hauling a black trash bag down the steps. The last thing he'd remembered hearing about George was that he had started up his own computer-graphics business. Maybe it had gone bust.

"George has important things to do." Patty's voice was sharp and she had a tight, odd smile on her face. "Maybe he'll grace us with his presence, and maybe not."

Parker saw Auntie Reiko trying to exchange a look with Uncle Min, but his uncle wouldn't look up from the tablecloth. "*Itadakimasu*," he said firmly, and everyone took their seats and responded in dutiful chorus, even Brad, "*Dozo*."

There was sukiyaki in an electric skillet, the orange extension cord snaking across the dining room table, just as Parker remembered from Sunday dinners after church. Auntie Reiko leaned over the pan, poking at the meat and the clear glossy noodles with extra-long chopsticks. Parker remembered a plastic plate with a duck on it that they had kept in the cabinet just for him. The blue hinged kiddie-chopsticks. He tried to remember how many years it had been since they had all sat around the table like this, his mother and father, aunt and uncle and cousins, lifting the curled meat out of the communal skillet, while the windows around them grew moist with steam.

Uncle Min's nose was the same shape as his own father's, a soft, short beak. They had the same wedge-shaped eyebrows too. Parker thought about the final months of his father's life: a chaotic seesawing between raging incoherence and disturbing, childlike affections. Parker never knew when his father might hurl his dinner to the floor or when he would hold out his jittering hand and whine, "Kiss."

His father had never kissed Parker before, not in his living memory. He had been gruff and distant, communicating mostly in disgusted grunts and a furious tossing of his head. "*Baka!*" he used to shout. *Stupid idiot.* There was not a sliver of kindness that Parker could dredge up from his childhood. All gifts, all warmth, every kiss was only from his mother. Or from Uncle.

Uncle Min was pouring sake into small white cups. Auntie had warmed it in the microwave. "I want to say toast for Parker," he said, his voice husky.

His aunt and Patty and Brad all lifted their little cups. The little boy waved a plastic cup of apple juice. "*Kampai*, Parker." *Kampai!* The heated sake coursed, clean and bright, through Parker's chest.

"Thank you, Uncle," Parker said, the heat of the drink strengthening his resolve. "I'm glad I can do this." This is my purpose, he thought. This is why I am here. He reached down, as had now become a habit, and rubbed his side. He wondered if he would have been able to do this for his own father.

Parker slept in his cousin George's room that night, surrounded by teenaged posters whose edges had begun to curl. There was no trace of the adult George, the slick guy who produced special-effects graphics for high-end clients like Pepsi and IBM. Parker lay between the clean, faded plaid bedsheets and wondered what his aunt and uncle's favored son had done. Nobody had mentioned his name again during dinner.

Parker slipped out of bed and walked to the kitchen in bare feet. There was a night-light glowing yellow over the stove. He dialed Joel's number, not caring that it was three in the morning in Denver. Joel didn't pick up, so Parker mumbled into the receiver, "Just wanted to let you know, I decided to do it. I'm at my uncle's in San Francisco. We check into the hospital tomorrow." He paused, wanting to say more, but he couldn't think of how to say it to a machine.

Parker woke up to the sound of Auntie Reiko's tapping on the doorframe. "*Ohayo gozaimasu,* Paka-chan. Big day today." Parker and Uncle were going to the hospital for a week of tests and hi-tech photographs, a careful mapping of their veins, the mysterious terrain of their livers' lobes. Before the first slice into flesh, they would see it all on computers, the plan of the entire medical procedure. Parker imagined the click of the mouse over his uncle's darkened liver, how it would lift and float into the little trashcan.

They ate breakfast in silence, bowls of *ochazuke*, hot tea over cold rice, with scrambled eggs on paper plates, and raisin toast. A soft wet grain of rice stuck to his Uncle's chin. As they listened to the drone of weather and traffic on the radio, a buzzer ripped through the kitchen. Auntie Reiko leapt to her feet. "Who—so early?"

And then her pained exclamation from the front door, "George!" Parker looked up to see a familiar face, but with a shining bald head and something sparkling and black in one earlobe. It was his cousin, but nearly unrecognizable. George wore a long black overcoat with delicate shoes and an expensive suit. Parker wondered for an instant, seeing the smooth bald head, if George had cancer, or a brain tumor, but he looked too healthy. He was carrying an armful of lilies wrapped in green waxed paper.

"Hi, Dad." George spoke to his father without looking at him, and then scraped a chair across the floor, straddling it backward. "Hey there, cuz." He narrowed his eyes for a second, and then flashed a brilliant, tooth-whitened smile. "You're a better man than I, Gunga Din."

Parker shrugged. "It worked out. Just luck that my blood matched and yours didn't."

A strange look passed over George's face—a microsecond of pity in his eyebrows. "Yeah."

Parker nodded toward his cousin's outfit. "Well, look at you, George. I guess life's been treating you fine." He hoped that George wouldn't ask about his job, shoestring editor at a monthly that was probably going to fold in a year.

"Well, yeah, the company is really taking off. We did twenty mil this quarter." George spoke with a distracted formality, and his eyes roamed from the ceiling to the floor and walls while he tilted back and forth on the kitchen chair.

"Is that right?" Parker had the urge to reach out and hold George still.

Auntie Reiko dug into the rice cooker with a wooden paddle. Her voice was high and wound up. "George, you want some *ochazuke*? Plenty here."

"No Ma, I already ate."

"So! Parker, are you seeing anyone? Got a girlfriend?" George looked pointedly at his parents. Uncle Min had put his head in his hands and Auntie was rubbing her fingers, shaking her head. George opened his wallet and showed Parker a photograph of a smiling young Asian woman in a ski jacket. The background was brilliant blue sky. "This is Nancy, Nancy Chu. You'll get an invitation to the wedding, next summer." George laughed. "*Shinajin*. Big banquet wedding, lots of good food." He folded the wallet into his coat. "You'll get an invitation. And you can bring a date." George stared at Parker with piercing eyes, the color of strong coffee.

Parker shrugged and dropped his gaze to the table. "I'm not seeing anyone right now." Joel had only been half a year, not long enough to introduce, just like all the others before him. He hadn't come out to his relatives, not really, not after his father had foamed and shouted, *baka* boy! *Kitanai!* Filthy.

George clapped his hands together. "So, Dad, you lucked out, didn't you?" There was steel in his voice. "Got old Parker here to give it up for you."

Auntie Reiko had backed away into the hallway with the telephone. She was calling the taxi company with a high urgency in her voice. "We need a ride to hospital."

Uncle Min lifted his head, wiped his mouth with a paper towel. "Parker is a good boy. Good nephew." He grunted and smiled with watery eyes at Parker.

"Yeah. He's the greatest." The two front legs of George's chair hit the floor with a sharp crack. "Only you know what, Dad? I would've done it for you." George leapt to his feet and was pacing the room now, his fine leather shoes slapping on the linoleum.

Uncle Min let out a small cry. "No."

Parker felt something slipping from him, his sense of understanding, his connectedness with the elderly man across the table. His being useful. Here he had been ready, ready for sacrifice, in his mind he was already stripped down and laid flat on a rock, his limbs bound with strips of leather. The hawks would be coming any day now, to tear his liver from his side, and deliver it, dripping, to his uncle. He was ready.

Uncle Min was shaking his head. "George. *Enough.*"

"No, Dad, I don't think it's enough. I don't think Cousin Parker here has heard enough. Not until you tell him that you wouldn't let Patty or me get our blood tested, wouldn't even let us talk to the doctors. And so now you've got this poor sucker here, and God help you both."

Parker blinked but still the room would not clear, would not slow its spinning. The sunlight from the glass suddenly hurt. His face twisted into a confused, helpless smile. "Wouldn't let you?" It was an enormous task to form each word.

George paced back and forth, his long black coat flapping like the wings of a bat. "That's right, cousin. That's right. We wanted to, Patty and I, because who *wouldn't* want to be able to do this for their very own father? But he said no. NO, he said, what about Patty's husband, what about Patty's child. Can't do this to them. And even me, I have this fi-an-cée, and I have this business; no, no, too much risk. Huh, Dad? So why don't we call Parker instead? He's healthy! He's athletic! As long as his blood checks out, he's the perfect candidate! He doesn't have any…" George abruptly stopped.

Uncle Min's face was nearly drained of its considerable color. He had turned his face to the window, his shoulders hunched around him.

George's face softened as he looked at Parker. He lifted his empty hands. "I had to tell you, cousin."

So that was why he had been chosen: not for being the favored nephew, for being beloved kin, but for being dispensable. For being alone. For being different.

Auntie Reiko stood in the kitchen doorway, her face wet, her mouth crumpled behind her hand. The bouquet that George had brought lay on the counter. The petals were soft and limp, drooping against the green paper.

Parker's mouth tried to say "Thank you," to George but his tongue lay fat and dense against his teeth. Was that the thing to say? Thank you? He stood up uncertainly.

His aunt's anguished voice ripped across the room. "Paka-chan! No! Not like George say!"

Parker drew a ragged breath and walked to where his uncle sat. He put his hand out, lightly, uncertainly, and touched the thin shoulder. He felt a faint ripple of pity pass through his fingers, and for a moment he thought of changing his mind, of saying *it's all right, it doesn't matter, I'll do it anyway*. But it wouldn't help things: wouldn't make Joel stay, wouldn't make Parker any less alone. The tiger kite had snapped its string and smashed to earth.

"Goodbye, Uncle."

He walked quickly to the hallway, to where his bag was already packed, ready for the hospital. The taxi was idling outside. He passed by his cousin on his way out, and saw that George's brown eyes were wet and bright. George bowed deeply, the front edges of his black overcoat brushing the floor. Parker leaned forward in return, and their two heads—one smooth and golden, one dark—touched briefly, then parted. &

(Untitled)

Simon Perchik

As if my lips have learned to weep
—after all these years
the evenings need more room

—my mouth is used to darkness
and goodbyes, kisses, though my eyes
were closed and now this spit trickles

place to place, covered with feathers
—it does no good, these sleeves
are soaked, held closer

than lifting your arms
and all that time your arms
filling with mist and your arms

seep through my lips—a great wave
unable to hold back
the hidden sea and your stillness.

ॐ

Last Visit

Kristin Camitta Zimet

Like a river in a long drought,
she is lying, low-pooled against pillows.
With the least crease beneath,
a riff passes through her. Drift
a hand downstream, you scrape
on clavicle and sternum, run aground
on the boulder in her belly.

Here is a sky so torn
you cannot breathe. But you hang
over her, a heron in the shallows,
claws prizing at pebbles
and slow-finned syllables,
for what still may slip
in the thin between air and earth.

Her eyes fill with you, flare
with a shine of water after sundown.
Love floods your chest like oxygen.
A cool and cradling come down
from a high country where the clouds
squall blessings, where the pulse
flows in extravagant thunder.

৪০

MacNamara's Ghost

Steve Fayer

The greatest moment in his life, my older brother told me, took place in a Brooklyn schoolyard in 1942. Sherwin was seven years old, playing catch with a kid named Maurice Rosen, when into the yard walks this seventeen-year-old hulk. Martin MacNamara was his name. I remember him even now with fear and trembling. A big, King Kong juvenile delinquent who is probably long dead, or serving a life term somewhere.

MacNamara steals Maurice's ball and begins to play catch with Sherwin. Back and forth, the pink spaldeen. My brother trapped in MacNamara's game. Maurice starts to cry. He has to be home and all that. And he wants his ball. He *begs* MacNamara for it. MacNamara says he'll kill him if he doesn't shut up. Maurice now begs my brother to throw him the ball. And they could both run, see, and escape from the big mick.

Finally, Sherwin turns. And throws Maurice Rosen the spaldeen, and Maurice tears through a hole in the wire fence wailing from the fear that MacNamara will be after them, carrying the fence and all of Brooklyn before him. But Sherwin has not moved. He stands there, sucking on his own tears. Watching the blood-red map of MacNamara. Waiting. Knees trembling. Think of it with your seven-year-old kid's mind. The son of a bitch's hands are around his neck. Sherwin falls unconscious onto the macadam. And MacNamara walks away, not giving a damn whether my brother Sherwin breathes, or expires.

All to make Maurice Rosen happy.

He told me it was the greatest moment in his life, twenty-five years later. After he got out of the first hospital. In the old neighborhood, we would have called the hospital a loony bin.

It was a new time in his life, Sherwin said. When he was going to face up to it all, and not be afraid of it, and tell it like it is—catch phrases he had borrowed from a young Greek Orthodox priest group therapist. I sat in on some of those sessions. And watched Sherwin encouraged to spill his guts. And felt bad for him. That he had to learn there that it was no shame not to have a sense of shame.

Something I do not happen to believe in.

But when Sherwin talked about MacNamara, it was roundtable time. Sherwin knighted for doing the good deed. For not running from the dragon. And Maurice Rosen like Guinevere, or the bard anonymous, would live to tell of it. Would hold high the magic spaldeen, would bounce it before the crowds and say, "Lo, the grail!" Rescued. Preserved. By Sherwin the Good. But better than that. By Sherwin the Courageous.

Can you believe it?

The greatest moment in his life.

The most awful moments in his life, the way he told them, so fast. It was like seeing Hieronymus Bosch spilling out of a high-speed press.

I think sometimes of the Kennedy kids. Growing up—up in Brookline— which by the sound of it was always in my mind a sister city to Brooklyn. Bobby, John, Joe sitting around the table with Old Joe and Rose, the mother and father instilling in those kids all the codes of behavior, of responsibility each to the other. All those martyrs. And Sherwin would have loved to have been there. To have breathed it all in. To have absorbed, by some Kennedy osmosis, the lion-heartedness. He would have died gladly in the Lincoln convertible in Dallas. Or on the floor of the hotel kitchen in Los Angeles. Or, most certainly, in Joe Junior's bomber in World War II.

How do I know all that? Because he told me.

And the greatest moment in his life? Standing up to MacNamara. The hulk darkening that Brooklyn afternoon. Little Sherwin throwing the ball away to Maurice Rosen. Probably throwing it chicken-armed at that. He was never much of a ball player, that brother of mine.

What the hell kind of victory is that?

The same as standing up to a freight train.

Sherwin with the shining lance, the silver spaldeen.

I hope, wherever he is off to, that they allow him the replay. Maurice crying, begging for justice and a way home. The toss. And then the hulk bearing down. And then the choke to unconsciousness. With all that good feeling inside of him, my brother Sherwin.

And then.

Maurice crying, begging for what is his. The silver spaldeen. And the fear in Sherwin. And then the decision. And the throw, chicken-armed or not, across the macadam, past the giant MacNamara's head. And the sun blotted out. And the terrible heat of MacNamara as he draws him in. The taste of his own tears as he goes under.

The good feeling.

And then, Maurice crying again. A kid without his very own spaldeen. And then the toss.

He had never cheated on anything—not since a test in school when he was fourteen—he told me once, when they had him tied up in the hospital bed, Sherwin rolled up in something that looked like an old navy hammock, talking about tests in school, and working a cash register, and his women. Because someday, he said, there would be a time when the question of his, Sherwin's, integrity would be of great importance.

He had such a low opinion of himself. That's why he was there. And such a high opinion of himself, against which to measure the low. And that's why he was there, too. I, by then, thought I knew my brother Sherwin pretty well.

You expecting to be in the history books some day? I said.

You're as crazy as I am, Sherwin said.

But I could tell he was pleased.

One night in Denmark. In Denmark? Yes, on one of those long escapes he granted himself, sometimes years-long, when he would be pissed off sufficiently at what he was doing, or whom he was doing it for, to drop out of sight. Sherwin renouncing the bag of happiness and the other goodies we are told lurk at the end of any of the American superhighways if we will only dig in when we get there, and stick it out.

Maybe he always felt he was better than what he was doing. Which, when you think about it, *can* lead to madness. He would work for years at an ordinary job in an ordinary place. And then, for one day, or one year, or two, he would disappear. And would show up again, like Allen Funt, when you least expected him. With a pilot's license in his pocket, or the papers of an able-bodied seaman. When we were kids and had bicycles, Sherwin would strike out for all corners of the borough of Brooklyn, and come back with tales of high adventure, of wanderings through cemeteries filled with ghostly marble, of a girl in a Flatbush playground who offered to kiss his pecker.

On *my* bicycle; I rarely if ever left the square block we called home. That is how different we were.

One night in Denmark, Sherwin, who had been drinking at bars along a beach some fifty kilometers north and west of Copenhagen, found himself closing a place called The Sunnyhouse, and being carried off in a convoy of rich kids and older Danish workers—carpenters, and eel fishermen, and foundrymen—all piled into MG roadsters, and ancient Ford Model A sedans, and Volkswagen pick-up trucks, and the sidecars of Nimbus motorcycles, bouncing along an unpaved, dirt road to a house in a forest. A beautiful house, all wood paneling, with great canted panes of glass all aimed for the sunrise.

It was *la dolce vita* north, Sherwin said later, in the hospital. Blonde maidens squatting to piss in the grass. A redhead running bare-breasted through the hallways. Members of the party raiding closets, dressing up in the clothes of the house, bathrobes, ridiculous old European underwear, a mechanic in a corset, cases of green-bottled Carlsberg Hof dragged across the beautiful varnished floors. It could make you cry, he said. Sherwin loved wood.

As my brother described it, there was a fire set in a great stone hearth, each log big as a dragon turd, and the burning flickered across all the beautiful faces and sweating torsos, and in all that crimson and blonde beauty, the people smelled like an old Brooklyn bar, he said, of sour sweat and spilled beer.

I remember sitting at his side, listening, and envying my older brother. First, that he was here first. A general principle. Then, that he was the freer spirit, even trussed up in that bed. That he could pull rank on me with one flash of Denmark. That he had in his head all these adventures that, to me, just might be worth the price of day-to-day sanity. Me, married to a Brooklyn brunette who never in her life had squatted to pee on any lawn that I can remember, who once, when we ran out of gas on the Garden State Parkway, hid herself in the shadow of the car and spread her skirts and made me not only look away but roll up the windows so that I and the two daughters, then aged two and five, could not hear.

When the sun rose that morning, they all stood worshipping it, necks stretched and backs arched under the canted windows, like hungry geese, Sherwin said. Then, a song. Half of them broke into a song and it sounded familiar to him. So he asked the beautiful blonde woman next to him, a Nordic ideal, he said, but with bad breath. What *is* that song?

The *Horst Wessel*, she said. With the old words, the good lyrics. And she started telling him about a special nursery school they had sponsored, to instill the old race principles, the hunger for purity.

Don't ask me what I did, Sherwin said.

I won't, I told him.

Nothing, he said.

When I think about my brother, I think there is a certain sort of bullshit that we live with. That the really good guys, the very best of them, never raised their hand. You know who they are. Jesus. Gandhi. King. But in our hearts, in the century just ended, we knew they were wrong. The *real* good guys were John Wayne, Erwin Rommel.

And our cousin Levi.

Levi is really our father's cousin, too old to be our contemporary. He grew up poor, like most immigrants' sons, and for economic reasons, mostly, he joined the cavalry in 1908 and fought with Pershing against Pancho Villa eight years later.

That ride across the Mexican frontier. He is a family legend who lived to almost one hundred, and settled in a town in Florida called Dania, painting watercolors, and drinking juice from raw vegetables and fresh fruit that he pulverized himself in a machine on his kitchen counter.

To stay young, he said. Five or six quarts a day.

I used to tell Sherwin that Levi probably never fired a shot. But Levi haunted my brother.

In the hospital, Sherwin started telling about another time, in Heidelberg, in the late fifties. He had been wandering all night in a rented Simca he had picked up in Paris, looking for the house of Frau Schmidt who had the only unrented bed in town.

There was a goddam music festival, he said. And to ask directions, he stopped at a bar, and walked into a reunion of the *Schutzstaffel*.

One of the Danish neo-Nazis had grabbed a dark-haired girl by the breasts and the crotch, coming at her from behind and lifting her off the floor. Sherwin had been talking to this girl earlier. She was not one of the group; like him, she had been swept along in the caravan from the bar near the beach.

There was this terrible dilemma, Sherwin said—about helping her. And there was the risk. The girl, for her part, did not hesitate. She waffled the drunken Dane, knocked him cold, the man going over backwards and bringing down a long wooden table as he fell.

She really hit him, Sherwin said. The man was unconscious, and she spat in his face. Then the girl sat down in Sherwin's lap and began to cry. And he tried to comfort her.

In Heidelberg? I asked.

No, damn it, he said. We are back in Denmark. It was *worse* in Denmark, he said.

The sun comes up awful early there, he said. Even in May. They paraded down to the beach, carrying cases of beer, drunks dressed in bathrobes and lace-up corsets, and the men pissing on each other. And on the beach, it was cold as hell, and Sherwin was curled up behind a dune with the girl, the heavy hitter. And they watched as some of the other girls stripped and went into the grey water, and some of the men did, too.

Vikings, he said.

Some of them were screwing in the dunes, behind the yellow scrub grass. And some had stayed back at the beautiful wooden house and were screwing there.

And my brother?

He asked me to undo one of the straps so he could smoke a cigarette. I told him that I couldn't, that they would throw me the hell out of there.

Verboten, he said loudly. *Forbudt*. And then raised his trussed-up legs in a stiff salute.

It would be a better story, Sherwin said, if I told you I tried to fuck her and couldn't.

Better than what?

Than what I did.

I lighted a cigarette for Sherwin, and held it for him.

The Greek priest had asked me to attend a group therapy session.

So we made love, Sherwin said, looking around at the circle of crazies and crazies' relatives, and at the priest who was nodding at him.

I *fucked* her, Sherwin said. No intakes of breath anywhere, just another crazy telling a crazy story.

Yes, the Greek priest said. It would be expected.

Sherwin was upset.

But would you have wanted it that way? he asked, first the priest and then all of them.

It was not love we made, he said. I hurt her. And afterwards she was crying because I had ripped her drawers.

Yes, the priest nodded.

Sherwin stared around him in amazement. Wouldn't it have been better, he asked, if I could *not* have gotten it up?

But that would have been punishing yourself, the priest said. Then a fifteen-year-old crazy who was there because she was starving herself so she would not look like a girl knelt down in front of her chair and threw up. The session ended, Sherwin still staring at us all. People started getting up, the seniles, and the kids, and some of the staff who were scattered around in civilian clothes.

My brother could not believe it. He would not stand up. Finally he turned to me and said, tell them about Maurice Rosen.

I was a little nauseated from watching the girl.

Tell them about the *spaldeen*, Sherwin commanded.

Years later, when Sherwin was all right, we were watching Levi grind beets in his machine in his little house in Dania. Levi was then eighty-one. Sherwin and I had driven down to Florida as in the old days, just the two of us, changing from driving to sleeping every two hundred miles, running for the sun like any other New Yorkers.

Hey, Levi, he said. What would you have done?

As if he were picking up on a conversation interrupted only a minute before.

There I was, Sherwin said, asking this goddamn kraut bartender where the hell was the house of Frau Schmidt, and the man is obviously scared of me, it being only a few years since they had lost the war. And there are all these men sitting at tables, big steins of beer in front of them, and then this one bastard stands up and walks over.

He has a long scar on his left cheek, Sherwin said. And his hair is grey-blonde, cropped short. And he stands right up to me. And he has bad breath. Almost everybody in Europe has, Sherwin said. And the son of a bitch tells me there is no Frau Schmidt. This is a private party, get out of here.

In the back of the room, Sherwin said, there is a man standing in front of a banner on the wall and he is carefully rolling it up. It has lightning insignia on it. But she is in this neighborhood, Sherwin tells him. They gave me directions at the railroad station. And as they talk, the quiet man in the scar-face keeps walking into him. And Sherwin keeps walking backwards. Finally, I realized what was going on, Sherwin said. So he took a step into the German.

Hard, Sherwin said.

And then? Levi asked, obviously puzzled.

Why then I walked out of there, Sherwin said.

Two years later, Levi is hanging off a ladder, touching up some painted trim on his house when Sherwin pulls into his driveway in a rented car from the Fort Lauderdale airport. It was pretty close to the end for Sherwin.

I flew all the way down here, Sherwin said. To ask you something.

Levi told me later he thought at first that Sherwin had come to borrow money. I am trying to re-create the scene, knowing both of them, my cavalry-rider second cousin and my older brother. Levi straightens up slowly and carefully wipes the brush against the edge of the can.

What would *you* have done? Sherwin asks.

About what? The old man stares at his cousin.

About scar-face, Sherwin says.

Levi is eighty-three now.

Capone?

Damn you, Sherwin says. I flew all the way down here and you play games with me.

Go find yourself a woman, maybe in Miami, Levi says.

Answer my question, Sherwin yells, still not out of the car, still talking through the open window.

About what?

About the fucking SS, Levi. *About* the bar filled with the SS in nineteen and fifty-eight.

SS? Cousin Levi ponders. Then the old man says the right thing for Levi, the wrong thing for my brother.

I would have killed them all, Levi says.

I never saw your brother again, my cousin Levi tells me at his eighty-fifth birthday party. He shakes his head, with the quiet pride the old ones have that they have survived. That they have survived even the generations that came after them.

I had forgotten all about it. That I am eleven and Sherwin is fifteen. That we are standing in the white-tiled doorway of a closed candy store in East New York, which is a section of Brooklyn, on an early Sunday morning, waiting for my Uncle Louie and my Aunt Sarah to pick us up and take us to Coney Island. And that there is this tough kid we've never seen before, maybe eighteen, who keeps hitting me. And Sherwin tries to push him off, and the tough kid hits him. And finally Sherwin just walks away, dragging me along, with this tough kid still pounding me on the back and on the head, and kicking me in the ass.

I had forgotten all about it, honest to God. Until Sherwin brings it all back, when he is forty-one and I am thirty-seven.

I let you down, he says.

Horseshit, I say. I don't even remember.

Sherwin down-drafted into the side of a mountain in New Hampshire in a glider he had been learning to fly all summer. Playing Joe, Junior. Probably.

My brother, a slain Mahatma for all the wrong reasons. Square man in a circular century. The license plates up there are white and green. The motto says, live free or die. And I try to calculate the effect of such advertising.

I am almost past all that bullshit of our seeing each other again. But I am sure that my older brother is not. And that someday, when I least expect it, I will turn up in his schoolyard. And there will be Maurice Rosen, standing in a corner by the wire fence, lower lip quivering. Maurice ready to piss his pants.

And Sherwin will be holding in his hands a pink rubber ball manufactured years ago, centuries ago, by the Spaulding Rubber Company. And he will say to me: Here, kid. You be MacNamara. And I will throw you the spaldeen.

And Maurice Rosen will be moving well away from me, a measured distance by the hole in the fence, his lower lip quivering, a phantom demanding love, and honor, and courage from my brother Sherwin. But not quite believing in him. And when I think of that moment, when I think that I have become MacNamara, I want to tell my older brother that it is all bullshit, that Maurice's spaldeen is not worth dying for. But I know that it is all too late. Standing once again in that century now dead, in Levi's dark shadow and in the crumpled fabric of Sherwin's glider, I know that I, too, am the victim of my brother's dreams. &

Ask Him If He Knows Jesus

Clarence Smith

A pair of snakes coiled up the shaft of a cross. This image appeared on a flyer in the student lounge—an advertisement for a medical clinic in Venezuela. "Volunteers needed for a rewarding experience in international health." I kept it folded in my pocket and a few days later, while studying pharmacology, used the back side to list the adverse effects of aspirin—thrombocytopenia, ulcers, hepatitis.

It wasn't clear to me why I called the phone number on the flyer. Since the death of my grandmother earlier that year, I'd begun to feel a kind of detachment. At times in the pathology lab, I had the somber but not unpleasant notion that the hands inside my latex gloves belonged to someone else. The two years of facts I'd learned so far in medical school had swelled into a leaking abscess.

The clinic in Venezuela, having received donations from a wealthy American church, would provide airfare and lodging for volunteers. I had to fill out an application which asked me to sign a statement affirming my belief in the infallibility of scripture. I signed because my grandmother had been a beach-lover and a Baptist, and I wanted her in Heaven searching for seashells. But in the margin beneath my signature I wrote an addendum explaining that contradictions precluded infallibility. The religious nature of the application attracted and repelled me at the same time. For years I'd been making occasional visits to various churches. I was beginning to realize that I enjoyed being ankle-deep in religion.

My application apparently found favor among the missionaries, and they sent a letter inviting me for the month of July, all expenses paid. As much as I'd hoped for some kind of rebuttal, the letter included no mention of my stance on the infallibility of scripture. It occurred to me that these missionaries might be more interested in practicing religion than discussing it. For a while I was almost embarrassed for having written the note.

After two planes and a three-hour cab, I arrived in the city of Merida, where the roads were clogged with decrepit American cars. Standing in the hotel parking lot, I had my first view of the Andes Mountains. I turned in a full circle, my head tilted back. In a nearby tree was an exotic bird with fiery colors. Uniformed gardeners were trimming foliage at the edge of the parking lot, some of them strapped with sawed-off shotguns.

There were twenty of us—physicians, medical students, nurses, dentists, and an optometrist. We boarded a red and white school bus that resembled a crumpled aluminum can that had been painstakingly straightened back out. The clinic itself was in a small mountain town half an hour away, and as we drove, encroaching verdure scraped the sides of the bus. We passed a settlement with dirty children in the shade of banana leaves, and huts made of corrugated steel, cinder block, and chicken wire. I saw a boulder that had been painted to look like a giant frog with purple and green spots.

I glanced at the white-haired man sitting beside me. His nametag read "George Mitchell, MD." He looked to be in his fifties, had blue eyes and a face sunned to the color of a grocery bag. When he gripped the seat-back in front of us, the sleeves of his scrubs tightened around his bulbous, vein-wrapped biceps. He had a leg stretched across the aisle.

"David Price," he said, reading my nametag, and I realized I should have introduced myself earlier. And then, as if resuming a long conversation, he said, "Only five percent of the people here are Christian."

"I thought this was a Catholic country."

"I'm not saying a devout Catholic can't be a Christian, but when you get to know these people, you'll understand they have no concept of God's love." He drew a penlight from his shirt pocket and flashed yellow circles on his palm. "For a lot of them, Jesus is just another statue."

Our bus heaved itself up an uneven road, past a motorcycle repair store, a grimy cafe, and an elementary school where the kids wore white shirts and blue pants. This road was like a cable keeping the town from sliding into the river. Stray dogs ran alongside our slow-moving wheels.

"Have you been here before?" I asked.

"No, but I went to Mexico last summer." After a pause he said, "When did you become a Christian?"

The question made me uncomfortable. "My dad was a serious believer, and my grandmother—my mom's mother—she was a Baptist."

"Tell me about your father."

"He took off when I was eight." I laughed before he could tell me how hard that must have been. "I see him now and then, and he's really happy I'm in med school."

The bus came to a stop, and across the street a crowd of maybe fifty waited outside what appeared to be our clinic. The older members of the crowd sat on a low, crumbling wall, and the rest formed something akin to a line on the narrow pathway running alongside the road. A group of children gazed curiously at our white faces in the bus's windows.

I watched as the first physician off our bus, his stethoscope around his neck, smiled his way into the crowd. A little girl reached out and touched his pants, as if there were communicable power in the blue scrubs.

The clinic was a converted church. The pews had been replaced with semiprivate stalls. I worked with Dr. Mitchell, who, it turned out, was a nephrologist. He insisted on praying aloud with each patient. He seemed to believe that God shared his interest in the kidney.

Late in the afternoon, he let me conduct an interview. The patient, Miguel, was an older man with a flannel shirt stretched tight over his paunch belly. A depiction of horses adorned his large belt buckle. He often felt thirsty and had to wake up at all hours to urinate. We didn't have the equipment to test his blood sugar, but I guessed he had diabetes, and Dr. Mitchell agreed.

"Can we pray for you?" Dr. Mitchell said as he balled his stethoscope between his hands.

The patient listened to the translation and said, "*Sí.*"

"David," he said to me, "why don't you pray for Miguel." He sounded like an anatomy instructor challenging me to make the first incision.

"All right," I said. I'd listened to Dr. Mitchell pray with four patients since morning, but I wasn't sure I knew how to do it. I had a distant memory of recitations at the dinner table when I was little. My father, before absconding with the preacher's wife, used to have me and my two brothers on our knees every night while he begged God—whom he called Daddy—to electrocute our family with the idea of eternity. After he left, my mother married a martial arts instructor.

Dr. Mitchell closed his eyes, waiting for me to pray. I stared at the top of his head. The sparse, evenly spaced strands of white hair reminded me of soil furrows after a light snow. I was nervous but, when I thought about it, the format of Dr. Mitchell's prayers seemed fairly straightforward. Thank God for something, apologize to God for a sin, and then ask God for something pragmatic.

Miguel wore a blank expression, and his calloused hands were folded between his thighs. His back straight, he sat in a cheap plastic chair. Our eyes met, and I quickly looked down at my sweating palms. I remembered learning all about the sympathetic nervous system. I recalled the biochemical pathways involved in sweating glands, dilating pupils, and various other features of anxiety.

"Lord," I said.

"*Dios,*" muttered the translator.

"Thank you for Miguel. Please forgive us for..." I paused, cudgeling my brain for a sin, and said, "Forgive us our great pride in medicine. And please lighten the burden of Miguel's polyuria."

"Excuse me," said the translator. "I will need a dictionary to translate that."

"Amen," I said. When I opened my eyes, Miguel was watching me. I'd made a fool of myself; Dr. Mitchell would give me a failing grade in prayer.

Miguel stood and hooked his thumbs through his belt. He told us about a man in town who needed to see the American doctors.

"He should come to the clinic," Dr. Mitchell said.

"But this man cannot walk," Miguel said through the translator. "He has no one to carry him."

"He needs to come to the clinic like everyone else." The nephrologist leaned back. The legs of his plastic chair bowed and scraped against the floor, on the verge of collapsing.

"The man's legs do not work. He was in a car wreck two years ago."

"We can't play favorites," Dr. Mitchell said, draping his stethoscope around his neck. "You saw the people out there." He gestured toward the front of the clinic. The crowd outside had grown since morning.

"He lives with his sister, but she works all day. She is..." The translator and Miguel discussed the meaning of a word. "The sister is a witch."

"He can ride to the clinic on her broomstick." Dr. Mitchell said this with a straight face, but then seemed relieved when the translator didn't understand. The doctor put his elbows on his knees, and his spine curved like a coastline.

Dr. Mitchell was the chief of medicine at a hospital in Atlanta. I could tell he was frustrated by the clinic's primitive methods of diagnosis. He was an expert in electrolyte physiology, but we lacked the technology to consider such things. There was no laboratory for analysis of blood and urine. His only sources of information were a translated interview and a physical exam. He caressed skin, palpated masses, and listened to organs through his stethoscope. He scrutinized every patient's fingernails. Our first day I watched him diagnose, with varying degrees of certainty, plantar fasciitis, diabetes, renal cell carcinoma, Goodpasture's syndrome, and four urinary tract infections. Urinary tract infections gave us a sense of accomplishment, because our meager pharmacy at least contained antibiotics. When a patient came in with bone pain, Dr. Mitchell asked questions about urine.

A few days later we saw a seven year-old boy without legs or testicles. When he sat in your lap, he wrapped his arms around your neck. His sun-wrinkled grandmother watched him with almond eyes while he walked around on his hands. We took pictures of him, and he smiled for all our cameras. He was a fraction of a person but he made legs seem cumbersome.

That afternoon, when the clinic closed for lunch, Dr. Mitchell and I sat in our cubicle. He told me we were going to visit the paralyzed man Miguel had mentioned.

I remembered how Dr. Mitchell had scoffed at the notion of a house call. "What made you change your mind?" I said.

"I'm happy to visit the man in my own spare time," he said, almost defensively, and I decided not to press the issue.

"If he's paraplegic, he'll probably have an indwelling catheter," Dr. Mitchell continued. He gazed at the pharmacy on the far side of the waiting area. He leaned forward in his chair and squinted, as if, from this distance, trying to read the label on a vial of pills. "We might need some Bactrim." He yawned, a fist covering his distended mouth, and I had the fleeting impression of a man hoping to mitigate his boredom with an afternoon adventure.

Dr. Mitchell didn't seem to mind when another physician and medical student joined us for the house call, but I found myself vaguely resentful of the extra company. The four of us followed our translator up the steep hill. This translator was Raul, a thin man with mirror sunglasses and hair that went from widow's peak to pony tail. His black boots were adorned with jangling spurs. He'd been converted by a previous group of medical missionaries, and now carried a small Bible in each back pocket. He looked back every so often to make sure we were keeping up. The climb was nothing to him.

Dr. Silas, a resident in dermatology, liked talking about the latest research. He said, "You can induce nerve tissue regeneration in adult lampreys."

"The lamprey's a good animal," Dr. Mitchell said. There were patches of sweat under his arms and down the middle of his back. He'd changed his nametag from "George" to "Jorge."

"And they've done it with rats at Johns Hopkins," Dr. Silas said.

"Amazing things are being done there." This was Todd, a medical student from Emory. Last night he'd shared his testimony with the staff, describing how he converted during his first year of medical school. He realized, while dissecting a cadaver, that he knew everything about his anatomy but nothing about his soul. When he began preaching to his classmates, the dean insisted on a psychiatric evaluation.

Some Mormons were walking in the opposite direction, and we exchanged tense greetings. They in their ties, and we in our scrubs—all of us fighting for the souls of Catholics.

"Forty-two people came to Christ yesterday," Todd said when the Mormons had passed. "The angels are celebrating in Heaven."

"It seems like they'd be sad," I said, "about all the people who didn't come to Christ."

The paralyzed man lived in a cinder-block hut at the end of a dirt trail. There were no buildings beyond it. A garbage heap seemed ready to subsume the small, dilapidated structure. It reminded me of phagocytosis, the process by which a cell engulfs surrounding debris.

Raul kicked a sun-bleached aluminum can and said, "You are a long way from laptop computers and that snake-charmer Marilyn Monroe." He gripped the bars of the hut's single window in which a bedsheet had been hung with duct tape and called, "*Señor* Camilo."

We could hear muffled words from within. The sheet fluttered—a flaccid sail briefly animated. Then a hand appeared and deposited a key on the windowsill. Raul took it and, before opening the door, peered around the side of the hut.

"I sense witchcraft," he whispered. He grabbed me by the wrist and flattened my hand against his chest.

"I have a gift," he added, "for detecting evil." I felt his racing pulse and almost believed him. He released my hand, just as the reflection of a mangy dog slithered over the silvery lenses of his sunglasses.

Inside, Camilo lay shirtless, his legs shrouded in bedsheets. He had acne scars and a dainty, well-trimmed mustache. His slack lips neglected a bead of saliva rolling toward his chin. Hanging from one of the bedposts was a plastic receptacle half-filled with watery urine. The catheter tube snaked down the bedpost and disappeared between the mattress and wall.

"*Hola*," said Dr. Mitchell. "We're doctors from the United States. It's nice to meet you."

Camilo nodded without making eye contact with any us. There were damp spots and crushed insects on the cement floor. A wheelchair was parked in the corner, but there was a step in the door and the terrain outside was rocky and overgrown. In an adjoining room was an unmade bed where his sister apparently slept. Raul said she worked all day and cared for her brother in the evening.

Dr. Silas looked at Raul and asked if Camilo had bedsores. I remembered my grandmother's bedsore, as deep as the nurse's finger.

"No," said Raul. He took off his sunglasses and slipped them into a breast pocket.

Dr. Mitchell asked if the catheter had caused an infection.

"No."

"Is he Catholic?" Todd asked.

"He has not gone to church in many years."

"These guys at Johns Hopkins," Dr. Silas said, looking at me and Todd, "their idea was that myelin induced regeneration, so they took this rat and cut its optic nerve."

Raul stepped into the sister's room, his nose twitching like an electrified frog-leg in a science experiment. I watched him through the doorway while Dr. Silas talked about the regeneration of a nerve at Johns Hopkins. Raul dropped to a knee and looked under the sister's bed. Closing his eyes, he mouthed a silent prayer.

"They wrapped it in the myelin of a sciatic nerve," Dr. Silas said, "and it grew back into the brain." He used his fist and index finger to illustrate the rat's nervous system.

At the end of the bed, Camilo's toes were curled and his feet were pointed downward like a ballerina's. With a slight jerking motion, one of them rotated outward.

"His foot moved," I said.

"It's normal to have muscle spasms," Dr. Mitchell said.

He scraped the tip of his penlight along the outer edge of Camilo's foot, which prompted the tendons to tighten reflexively, pulling the toes upward. Then he looked Camilo in the face and asked, "Does it hurt when your foot moves?" He repeated the question for Raul, who had just returned from the sister's bedroom.

"*Sí*," Camilo said.

Dr. Mitchell placed his fingers on Camilo's wrist and, after feeling the pulse, stood beside the bed with his hands on his hips. There was a period of silence. I wanted him to give Camilo a thorough examination. He represented the best of modern medicine, and I believed he would somehow make Camilo's life better.

Camilo reached for an envelope on his bedside table. He held it in a trembling hand and spoke briefly to Raul.

"He's saving money for a trip to Cuba," Raul said. "The surgeons there will cure him."

In the envelope was a passport substantiating Camilo's plans.

"Many great doctors are in Cuba," Raul said with a hint of pride. "You heard about the Americans putting razor blades in Castro's breakfast? The surgeons stitched up his tongue with silk thread."

"I don't know of any research coming out of Cuba," Dr. Silas said.

"They do all kinds of research," Dr. Mitchell said, "and ethics are a top priority, I'm sure." He cleared his throat, coughing up the residue of his sarcasm.

Camilo nudged me with his passport. He wanted me to look at it. It was brand new, and probably the only object here that he valued. Someone was going to stamp a cure onto one of its pages. I passed it to Dr. Mitchell, who bent it by its edges until the pages fluttered back into place.

Looking at Raul, Dr. Mitchell said, "Ask him if he knows Jesus."

Raul explained that some Jehovah's witnesses had come just last week.

"He needs to stay away from Jehovah's witnesses," Dr. Mitchell said. "They're morons."

Raul said, "Is a moron the same as a son of a bitch?"

"No," said Dr. Mitchell.

Todd told Camilo a story from the Bible. A group of believers brought a paralytic to see Jesus. A crowd blocked the doorway, so they lowered the man with ropes through an opening in the roof. After Jesus healed him, the man triumphantly carried his mat into the street. Some day, Camilo might carry his wheelchair.

Raul paused in his translation, looked thoughtful for a moment, then added, "Wheelchairs are very heavy."

"Just tell him," Todd said, annoyed.

I wished Todd had chosen a different Bible story, something more ambiguous, like the part where Abraham nearly murdered his own son. For some reason, I was embarrassed to hear about Christ healing a paralytic.

"You'll walk in Heaven one day if you accept Jesus Christ as your personal Lord and Savior," Todd said. "Would you like to do that?"

"*Si.*"

Todd seemed as if he would preach for hours, promising Camilo an alternative to Cuban surgery. It was easy for him to evangelize, being insulated by language. While Raul translated, Todd stood there mapping out his next sentence. I remembered how, when I was young and going to church with my family, religion had suggested a comforting mystery. Now the words were worn out, as if they meant something different to everyone who used them.

"Streets paved with gold," Todd intoned, "and you walking around."

"*Si.*"

Dr. Mitchell checked the time. His watch glinted in a beam of sunlight coming through a small hole in the roof. On the wall a broken clock was illustrated with a nativity scene. The paralyzed second hand divided Mary's head and nimbus.

Todd moved closer to the bed. "Would you like to accept Jesus as your personal Lord and Savior?"

"*Si.*"

"He's just telling you what you want to hear," I said. My voice echoed strangely, as if it were searching the room for a place to lie down. "Can't you see that? He'd commit his soul to Notre Dame football if you asked him to."

"Camilo," Todd said, ignoring me, "do you acknowledge that you're a sinner?"

"Maybe we should pray," Dr. Mitchell said sharply, laying a hand on Todd's shoulder.

Stepping back from the bed, Todd had a look of despair, as if suddenly realizing, after countless chest compressions, that his patient was long dead.

Dr. Mitchell stared at me, and I feared he would request another of my untranslatable prayers. But instead he said, "Is there anything you'd like to tell Camilo before we pray?"

I looked at Camilo, whose gaze was directed somewhere safe. After a moment I said, "No."

Dr. Mitchell's eyes swiveled over each of us before targeting Camilo. "What we're going to do is lay our hands on this poor man's legs."

His nostrils flared, as if relishing the scent of Christ's blood on Camilo.

We knelt around the bed. The stone floor was cold against my knees.

Dr. Mitchell began, "Gracious, almighty, heavenly Father."

"*Dios*," said Raul.

"Thank you for our brother Camilo. He has shown us our limitations. If we had one iota of faith…"

"I'm having trouble translating that."

"It's something really small."

"I will say the faith of a mustard seed." He said it.

"I just want Camilo to know that even a small amount of faith is enough to make him walk."

"I see," Raul said. "Perhaps I should pray as well?"

Our hands were draped over Camilo's dead legs. The patient looked me in the eyes for the first time.

As Raul prayed, he squeezed his eyes shut, perhaps to see God better. I didn't understand anything he said, but I felt as though his prayer contained something more than the meaning of its words. I became uncomfortable and shifted my weight from one knee to the other.

Camilo's leg twitched beneath my hand. I'd hoped he would stand up, but then, after the prayer, I was actually relieved to see him still paralyzed, to see that things were still the same even though we had prayed. We left one of Raul's Bibles on the bedside table, amid canisters of antiseptic.

On the way back to the clinic I caught up to Raul and asked him what he'd seen in the sister's bedroom. He said a pentagram was painted under the bed, sprinkled with blood, probably that of a chicken. "You see," he said, "there are demons everywhere."

That night I went to fill my canteen with potable water from an outdoor dispenser, and as I strolled back to my room, I saw a pair of Catholic priests, heads bowed, pacing the lawn. The one closest to me fingered a loop of rosary beads. I passed a rusty swing set which, incongruously, had been built in the hotel's parking lot. The slide ran directly into the grill of an old Ford. Dr. Mitchell sat in one of the swings, its chains squeaking. His slight motion suggested a settling pendulum, but his bare feet kept him moving.

"How did you feel about Camilo today?" he asked.

"I wish he'd gotten up and walked." Sitting in the next swing, I felt the chains tighten in my hands.

"What would you have done?" Dr. Mitchell said. A hotel employee slouched across the parking lot with a shotgun. "If he'd walked, it would have been a miracle. You can't just ignore a miracle."

"That's not something I'd ignore." I nodded toward the priests on the nearby lawn and said, "Maybe I'd become one of them."

"A real miracle destroys your faith," the doctor said, "because when you see one, you have no choice but to believe."

"I'm not sure I even know what a miracle is."

"A miracle is a club to the back of the knees."

One of the priests, having finished praying, walked into the well-lit hotel entrance. Though I couldn't see his face, something about him told me he was smiling.

The next morning, Camilo's sister, the witch, came to the clinic to thank us for the modern medical treatment that had restored her brother's legs. She said he wriggled his toes not long after waking. He slid one foot to the floor, and then the other. He tried to stand, but his atrophied legs weren't strong enough to carry him. When we explained we'd done nothing but pray, she crossed herself and announced a miracle.

We didn't believe her. But then Camilo himself arrived with two neighbors supporting him under the arms. Todd dropped to his knees shouting praises to God. Tears began spilling out of his eyes. He crawled across the cement floor, gripped Camilo by the ankles, and kissed his feet. Apathy had been chiseled into the smooth granite of Camilo's face, but I could discern the beginnings of a smile. The smile came in parts, as if each facial muscle had to remember its role.

Dr. Mitchell and I had been interviewing a teenager one month pregnant when Camilo arrived. The three of us stopped to watch Todd embrace his way up Camilo's body. It seemed as though he wept from desire, from wanting more than anything for the miracle to be real. I could tell that Todd was trying desperately to incorporate the miracle into his personal Venezuela story. After releasing Camilo, he stood up straight, wiped his tears, and then, in a courteous fashion, shook Camilo's hand as if to welcome him back into the ambulatory world. The two turned and presented broad smiles to their audience.

Dragging a chair from our cubicle, Dr. Mitchell invited Camilo to sit down. He rapped Camilo's legs with the bell of his stethoscope, eliciting normal patellar and ankle reflexes. Then he removed Camilo's shoes and socks to inspect his bare feet. Dr. Mitchell concluded his exam with a shrug. This man's legs are normal, his expression seemed to say, just withered by inactivity.

One of the nurses pulled out her guitar and began singing "Hark the Herald." Other members of the staff joined in. I saw Dr. Silas place his arm around the optometrist's shoulders and, swaying side to side, the two of them poured their voices into the mix. The Venezuelans who couldn't sing in English hummed along with the tune. The staff aggregated around Camilo, who smiled and said nothing. I saw Raul leaning into the music, his hands in his back pockets. His mouth was clenched shut, as if resisting an urge that threatened to overwhelm him.

I slipped out the back door. There was an enclosed space behind the church, where some dogs were nosing through a pile of garbage. I wanted to believe the miracle had been a hoax. I could hear the celebration building inside. After a while the door opened, disgorging Dr. Mitchell with a surge of music. We stood there and watched a dog jam its snout into a greasy paper bag. Dr. Mitchell's stethoscope was clamped to his neck, the bell dangling over his belly. "It's a miracle," he said, and I wondered if God was mocking us. &

The Well

Jan Lee Ande

It is written that in the days of Abraham the Father,
the Philistines filled up his wells with rock and mud.

So Isaac's servants dug in the valley and found there
founts of flowing water, and before one, built an altar.

If a man lifts a thirty kilogram bucket from a well
one hundred meters deep, how much work does he do?

Let f^1 equal the gravitational force. Note the work
is positive, that the man expends energy lifting the bucket.

What happens when a child falls twenty two feet
down an abandoned wellshaft in the heartland?

Why does the rescuer who labored two and a half days
to bring her back into the light, take his own life?

Note the work is negative, that the gravitational field
surrounding the bucket gains energy as it is lifted.

How far down in the mingled wellspring of creativity
do syllables abide? Is it so dark near the quickening

water that blue stars shine and then set, taking
their blackened light back into the fountainhead?

&

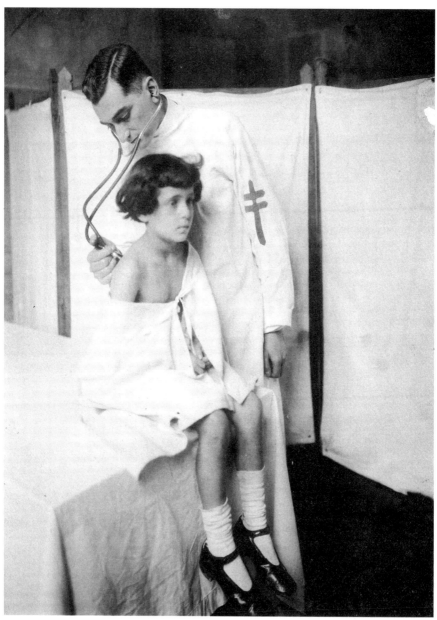

Chest doctor examining a child, circa 1919. The Cross of Lorraine on the doctor's jacket was the symbol of the NY Lung Association. Courtesy of Bellevue Hospital Archives: Chest Collection.

A Room With No Door

Megan Corazza

I remember my father's face getting blacker, and how his weak coughing would fleck the bedcovers with blood. My older sister Anju and I were secretly happy that he was never hungry. When he only took a few handfuls of the rice and turned away, my mother always tried to make him eat more. He would make angry noises through his coughing, and then she would push the plate towards our eager hands with her trembling ones.

I realize now that, as an eight-year-old boy, I had spent my entire life watching my father die. I couldn't remember it's ever having been different, but Anju could, and she told me the story of the first doctors and hospitals in Kathmandu. She said that the outside of his eyes had gone from being white to looking like the yolk of an egg. Anju said that one woman, who always brought her saris and blouses to my father for stitching, told my mother about medicines that would make his eyes clear again. The lady gave us some money to take him to a hospital. Even now, using the urinal in the morning makes me think of Anju and the games she would play with us during the long, hot days of the monsoon season in Nepal. "Let's think of things that are yellow like *baa's* eyes," she would say to our three year-old sister, Chandra, and me. Possibilities were everywhere. Bananas, pee, the huge letters I couldn't yet read on roadside billboards, the sun, bolts of cloth lined up neatly behind my father's sewing machine, and the packages of Coconut Crunchies at BishnuAuntie's store. Chandra would just point to the four glass jars of spices on a high shelf against the gray concrete wall.

They kept our father at the hospital until his eyes were white again, and then he came home. But people stopped bringing their saris to him anyway because he was staining the cloth when he coughed. Mother told Anju to watch me and Chandra while they went to a different hospital. When they came back, they had a small picture that showed his ribs and heart. His lungs were two dark empty spaces that looked as if they had spiderwebs strung in them. They also brought back shiny packets of medicines, and Anju used to push pills through the thin silver skin and let Chandra and me play with them on the floor.

For eight years he took the medicines. When I was eight years old and big enough to roll an old bike tire through the streets with a stick, the picture of the spiderwebs in my father hung next to a picture of Ganesh, the man with an elephant's head. When I was ten years old and came in sticky from games of cricket with some other boys, my father's scratched, blue and white picture hung next to a crooked painting of Jesus, naked and stretched on a wooden beam. "Without the church ladies," my mother told us sternly, "your father would not have any medicine." Anju and I begrudged him this; he had medicine but we lost most of our friends. It was bad enough to have a sick father; nobody would sit where he used to sit at the tea shop, and when we played in the street, mothers with thin, tinkling glass bracelets on their arms would grab our friends, dragging them away. When the women from church would come over to pray in our room, their foreheads scrubbed free of the traditional red powder, even our few remaining friends would shout and point from a distance, kicking loose rocks at them.

Sometimes my father would get better, but then one of us would get sick, and he would start to cough all over again. When Chandra was four, she started coughing at night. This time, she was sick at the same time as my father, and mother said they couldn't both get medicines, or there would be no rice or lentils for the rest of us. While my father and I pushed Chandra's ashes and the unburnt wood into the river, my mother looked away, smoothed her hair, re-tucked her sari, and avoided the burning eyes of Anju and me.

A visit from the doctor always began with my mother's voice, raspy but loud, coming from the single window in our room.

"Prakash!"

I would hand the bat to my friend, Pramod, and let my sandals flap loudly as I trudged up to the third story of our apartment building, dragging my hand along the crumbling walls in the dim hallway. My fingertips would bounce from the gritty concrete of the walls to the rough wood of each of our neighbors' doors. After my hands had gone across seven doors, I knew that our room was next. Where there should have been a door, there was nothing but a six inch-high scrap of tin that Anju had put on the ground to keep the mice out.

"Prakash, put on your long pants and your green shirt! The doctor is coming soon, hurry! Anju, hold the baby!" I knelt down to pull my box out from under the bed we all shared. Anju sat down on the edge of the bed, bouncing our new baby sister, Jhoti. My mother put on her necklace, straightened her sweater near her wrists, and pushed the stove as far as possible into the corner. She wiped the spit from my father's face, which was as black as the bottom of a pot, and pulled the covers up to his chin. He shook his head and coughed, trying to tell her that he was too hot already, but she'd already turned away and was unwrapping the dirty shawl around Jhoti. There was no pee, so she wrapped the baby up again and handed her back to Anju. Taking a step to the doorway, she bent down to arrange all of our *chupples* in pairs.

"*Namaste, didi!*" My mother straightened quickly, surprised by the doctor's quiet approach and deep voice. She smiled and folded her hands together. She stepped to the side and told us to stand up so that the good doctor could look at father. He looked at Anju and me, touched the bottom of the baby's foot, and then sat down on the bed. He held my father's wrists and asked him questions while my mother pulled the stove from the corner and began to heat up some milk. She unwrapped the edge of her sari, untied one corner, and, with a sharp look, handed me four rupees.

I ran to BishnuAuntie's store on the corner, feeling as rich as the doctor. I didn't look at my friend Pramod when he shouted at me from the alley. I remember stopping a little way from the store, to practice reading the numbers on the coins. I didn't know the words, but they looked like the inside of Pramod's school books. I could have walked up to the counter and asked for an egg. I could have pointed at the candy jar and gotten eight White Rabbits. A whole package of Coconut Crunchies. But at the counter, I just stood and looked up at BishnuAuntie. She didn't even turn to me.

"Prakash, stop staring," she said. "Leave me alone; I'm busy!" When she did finally look at me, she saw the rupees I was holding out.

"One packet of tea, please."

She laughed like the first water out of the pump, and reached towards the back shelf. "The doctor again? I don't know how your mother can afford him."

I didn't answer. Taking the small plastic packet and leaving the shiny coins, I ran back home.

I handed the packet to my mother and stepped back over the tin in the empty doorway to watch the doctor from a distance. He didn't look the same as us; he was tall and his skin was light brown, instead of looking like us—like burnt *chapatis*. He told us he was from India, and I used to imagine how the streets of India must be full of tall, calm, quiet men with friendly eyes, instead of the dirty, crowded streets of Nepal filled with shouting men and dogs with bleeding sores.

My father was lying on his stomach, hanging his head over the edge of the bed, and coughing. Coughing is hard to do for eight years, so by the end the doctor had to help him. My father made small sounds like a cat, and the doctor hit his back, up and down and up and down. Green spit with bloody bubbles dripped slowly out of my father's mouth, and the doctor collected it in the bowl that he brought every time. The doctor always put a lid on the bowl and took it away with him, telling us that it would help other people not to get sick. After a while, the doctor helped my father roll back over onto the far side of the bed. Mother turned away from the wall with a steaming cup of tea. He handed me the silver tubes he used for listening to father's heart, and motioned for my mother to follow him outside to the roof, which was through the empty doorway at the end of the hall.

This was our favorite part. I stepped back over the scrap of tin in the doorway and stood next to Anju. She held the silver disk below her throat, and I carefully put the long tubes up next to my ears. The sound was like the big trucks starting up in the mornings, slow and throbbing. Anju said mine sounded like water being poured into a bowl. Mother and the doctor were gone for a long time, so we listened to Jhoti's heart, too, but all we could hear through the tubes was her breathing, which was as loud as our father's as we'd try to sleep at night. Suddenly they reappeared from the roof.

"Prakash, Anju, say goodbye to the doctor. Jhoti, can you say goodbye?"

"Bye bye," said Anju, waving Jhoti's tiny hand.

I handed the tubes back to the doctor, watching his smooth, long fingers curl around the dirty fingerprints we had left on the silver. He looked sad and walked slowly away, looking back once more at my mother from the end of the dark hallway. "What did he say, *aamaa*?" I asked. Mother dipped her hand in a bowl of water and began to scrub the milk that had burned to the side of the pan. Her cracked lips opened and closed with no words, and then she started to clean the doctor's cup.

"Anju." Mother's voice was quiet, but it was a choking kind of quiet that made Anju stop playing with the baby and listen. "Prakash, Anju, the doctor said that your father's sickness has gotten very strong. No one can visit him anymore, and it is better if we are not in the house. You have to sleep outside for a while."

Two months after my father died, the landlord became bolder. Before, he used to just peek in at our room and tell my father that his coughing was making the neighbors angry. Now, he told my mother she couldn't hang up clothes to dry on the roof because the sickness was still in our room. He kicked the *chupples* that were lined up outside the doorway, and threatened not to rent the room to us. He burned the bench that my father used to sit on outside.

My father died in the rainy season, and by the time the fields were full of dry, hard clods, fourteen year-old Anju had left, and there was more room on the bed. A man from India named Kanchha, with shiny hair and nice shoes, had started coming to visit her. He never talked to Jhoti or me; he only spoke a few words with my mother and always handed her something before holding Anju by the shoulder and taking her outside. They talked on the roof while mother sat inside looking at the picture of the spiderwebs that were under my father's ribs. Right before my father died, we could see the bones underneath his skin, and his heart beating in the middle, and he looked like that picture.

I was playing one day between the houses stacked high and close, like the bowls of curd that men sell in the morning, and I heard the neighbors say my mother let Anju go with Kanchha because then we could eat twice a day. They said that my mother must know that India was not very nice, and my sister would probably get sick from all the men, the kind of sickness doctors couldn't heal you from, and wasn't it sad that a girl as sweet as Anju was tricked into thinking she would be a bride. One of them rubbed at the clothes she was washing with blue soap, scrubbed them furiously against a stone, and said that she hoped Kanchha didn't think he could come back for their daughters, too. I got angry and went over to them. I told them what my mother told me, about Kanchha asking her if he could marry Anju, and how excited Anju was, and how we would go down to visit them in India someday.

When I went home, I asked my mother why we didn't use the money that Kanchha gave her to go down to the wedding. She said that she got sick on buses, and that I probably would, too. Wasn't I happy, she asked, that I had my own schoolbooks and a uniform now?

When I was eleven, baby Jhoti started to breathe like an old man, so I told my mother to take her to the hospital. She dug out her nicest sari from the bottom of the wooden cupboard, put on sandals with high heels and wrapped the baby tight around her back. I went with them to keep my mother from being scared of the doctors. The doctor listened to the baby's heart, and then asked if there was anybody in the house with the coughing sickness. My mother said no. I said there used to be. I said my father and my sister both died after getting sick. The doctor's face turned the color of BishnuAuntie's eggplants, and he looked at my mother. Don't you know, he said, that this sickness is passed from person to person? You should not be sleeping in the same room, you should not share the same food. You should keep all your windows open and make sure the sun dries your clothes. He looked at me. If you do not do these things, Prakash will be the next. He is already skinny and his eyes are not clear.

My mother wiped her eyes and said she had heard these things, but didn't know if they were true or not. I just played with the silver band around Jhoti's ankle.

I told my mother that I would quit school so that we could pay for the baby's medicine, but she started crying. She said that the women who came to church in silk saris were helping. I saw them give her a plastic bag every week, full of milk powder and rice. And she told me that Mitudidi from the church invited her over every morning while I was gone at school and they would have a big meal. I was happy. Before, I never knew why she didn't eat with me.

I came home from school, and my mother was sitting alone on the bed. There were rocks holding down the edge of her sari as it hung out the window, drying. She was coughing. I put my uniform in the box under the bed, and she held out a *manna* of peanuts, wrapped in newspaper.

"*Aamaa!* Thank you," I said. "Here, share with me."

She waved her hand and turned away coughing. "Eat, Prakash. I have something to tell you."

"Did you hear from Anju?" I asked through a mouthful, shells piling up on the straw mat.

"I am getting sick, Prakash. I have been thinking about what the doctor says, and your eyes, and your father… you need to tell Mitudidi and the other church ladies not to come over. Pramod can't visit either. And… you need to sleep outside again."

From the roof, I heard a cup smash on the floor. My eyes opened and I was awake, staring into the darkness.

"No," a man's voice hissed in an angry whisper. "No! Your face is getting black, like the bottom of my foot. You offer yourself to me?! Your neck is thin, your children spit green all around my building, and your clothes smell like piss. You've already made your husband and children rot! You have no pleasure to give; you are not worth money."

There was a scuffling and a clatter as someone tripped over the tin at the bottom of the doorway. Quick, heavy footsteps faded down the hallway. The baby started crying. Then there was only the sound of the faraway truck horns and my own heart, like I was listening to it with the doctor's silver tubes.

That night I lay quietly on my grass mat on the roof, looking up at the sky and wondering how the moon felt when it was full. The barking of dogs and the hiss of pressure cookers and the sharp voices of women filled the small spaces between buildings, and I pulled the blanket tight around my neck. Doors shut, taxis stuttered to a stop, and mice ran across the sagging line where the corn hung drying. I wondered about Anju and Kanchha's life in India. In school we saw pictures of huge white temples in India, camels in the street, elephants, and the ocean. I would love to see the ocean. ∞

Cemetery Plums

Jim Tolan

One who would offer ripe fruit to the dead
as if knowing their desires, as if believing
desires still lived in them, would know
how tangible remains the memory of its juice

across the mouth and chin and sliding
along the tongue. Do not be misled.
The dead miss life more than we miss them,
their loss more than equal to our forgetting

and our grief. And a bowl of fruit offered
in their name returns to them as the memory
of a mouth rapt in joy around moist and living
flesh. Who among the dead does not long

for the sun-wet meat of smooth-skinned plums,
the bitter sweetness of each pitted heart?

&

Youthful Acts of Charity

Marylee MacDonald

The ashtray of the little Fiat overflowed with snuffed-out butts that spilled onto the floor at every hairpin turn, while the driver, Harun, swayed in time to a Turkish singer clanging finger cymbals. Bonnie Cross, fifty-five, gripped the handle on the passenger door to keep from lunging sideways. Her breasts and stomach jiggled. She looked down. Ivory buttons stretched the buttonholes and she hoped the thread was strong; she hadn't remembered to bring a safety pin, even though this blouse was an oldie, back when size 18 still fit. Suction held her thighs to the leather seat.

"I'm sooo hot," she said.

Harun, half her age, threw open the vents. Her skirt ballooned, and his eyes rolled like marbles, dropping in her lap.

"Why is it, men think they're God's gift to women?" she said, punching down the faded batik of her skirt. "Or in your case, Allah's gift?"

"But is true, don't you think? Womans need man, and man womans."

"Right, they do." Looking out to sea, she saw another cruise ship, similar to her own. She had come here on a singles trip, two weeks in the Mediterranean. She was glad to have hired this waiter, who was squinting against the glare now, to show her "the real Turkey." Harun's long fingers on the gearshift reminded her of that old game: scissors, paper, rock. An adorable curl bounced on his forehead. Somewhere in his genetic line stood a Mongol warrior; she could practically hear hooves beating across the steppes. In less than a week, she'd be back in her Chicago office—the padded cubicle, pizza dinners, and PowerPoint presentations. Hospital consulting was no kind of life.

They arrived in a village a few miles from the coast where Harun had arranged for her to meet the locals. His great uncle, a stooped farmer in a black beret, led them upstairs, and the great aunt, in harem pants and headscarf, motioned Bonnie to a seat on the carpet. Out came a platter of appetizers. As Bonnie filled her plate and bit into a stuffed grape leaf, oil dribbled down her chin. Making a grab for Harun's pants, the great-uncle turned the boy's pocket inside out. "*Cebimde para yokken, siz hic bir sey istemiyeceksiniz,*" the old man said.

Harun blushed. "He say next time, come with money in mine pocket. Is family joke. Mine father not rich man like great-uncle."

Bonnie glanced at the small portions the others had taken; she was ready for seconds. "Is your father poor?" she said.

He shrugged. "Born poor. Die poor."

Mea culpa, Harun. Eyes cast down, he did penance for her overeating, nodding while the great-aunt fiddled with the knot in her scarf and told long, musical stories. Occasionally, Harun muttered a low "*Evet.*" If the great-uncle laughed, beating his beret against his knee, Harun laughed, too. "*Hayir! Hayir!*" he said, his voice rising. The old people were reminiscing about the time of Ataturk, Harun told her. Back then, the great-uncle and Harun's father had kidnapped a beautiful young woman, tied her to a donkey, and carried her down to the grandfather's compound, fighting off her father and brothers with guns.

"How barbaric," Bonnie said.

"Make mine mother many tears," Harun said.

"Your mother?"

Harun raised his eyebrows and motioned toward the door. Next stop on the itinerary: a swim in the Mediterranean. He took her hand and helped her from the floor without the slightest strain or smirk. She struggled up and her face tingled when his thumb pressed her fingers.

Dodging wet laundry in the courtyard, she said, "Didn't your mother hate him?"

"Not for long." He closed the gate.

As the car spun out, Bonnie saw a gray donkey with flattened ears tethered to an olive tree. "But she was kidnapped."

He was silent for moment. "Turkish men know how make woman happy."

"And what do Turkish women say?"

"She have fourteen children," he said smiling. "I baby."

A rutted, gravel road twisted steeply down to the cove at Claros, and Harun edged the car into the first turn, his eyes following the zigzags. The car slid on two wheels, and the steering column chattered as they spun downhill, careening madly over the washboards. Toad's Wild Ride, she thought, exhilarated. The car rolled to a stop by a half-finished bathhouse, where she saw a gangly pole with a rusty showerhead and a windbreak of weather-beaten cypress.

"*Allahu akbar!*" Harun's head dropped against the steering wheel.

"That was superb," she said.

He unstuck his hands. "I hope I not have trouble to get it up."

She took a deep breath. Her heart began to race, and she was about to say, half-seriously, don't worry, I can help.

"Is little joke," he said. "Easier for car go up than come down."

Vaguely annoyed, Bonnie stayed by the car, watching him amble down to the water, turning over rocks with his toe. With the hatchback open, she peeled off her clothes and, grabbing a handful of belly, longed for a steak knife to trim three decades from the lean girl underneath. She glanced back at the chaparral-covered cliffs; they reminded her of Big Sur and Esalen where she'd soaked in the hot baths and studied massage years ago. Fritz Perls, the white-haired guru of the inner life must be long dead. What had become of the burnt-out therapists with droopy muscles and baggy skin, begging for a piece of her young ass? Ah, what youthful acts of charity, loving them. Now here she was, equally ridiculous, breasts bulging out—fat, white melons—thinking, my face looks young. Giving the elastic around her legs a final snap, Bonnie sighed, thankful for the tummy panel and the slimming effect of black. A beach-towel sarong hid the dimpled cellulite.

When she emerged from the bushes, Harun sat fully dressed on a picnic table, staring at the horizon. With his cigarette, he made a circular motion. She scrunched up her face and walked across the rocky beach toward the surf.

"What you do? I say turn around. You turn around, please."

Bonnie stuck out her tongue and pulled the towel over her shoulders.

"You not swim with towel. Drop towel, I say." He motioned again, eyes smoldering.

She dropped the towel.

"Beautiful." He made an hourglass. "I admire women of your body type."

"Bullshit."

"No, really. Well-fed womans have lots of, lots of good spirit."

She rolled her eyes and took mincing steps to the water. Shards of ice pierced her ankles. Gasping, she staggered out.

Harun pulled off his shirt and rolled up the legs of his pants. He had a slight frame, limbs sinewy and lean. Harun, a howling name, like the wind that blew straight into her ears. He unzipped.

"What are you doing?" she asked.

"Shining." He pointed up. "I take sun."

"Didn't you bring a suit?"

He shrugged. "I forgot."

"You can swim in your pants." *Long* pants, she meant.

"I don't want swim," he said. "Just take sun."

His trousers dropped. He looked down at the puddle of clothes and stepped onto the stones. For a second, she thought he had on little girl's underpants. Sage green and iridescent, his briefs had thin elastic around the top. No fly. He hiked up the sides to cover his bony hips. Standing next to her, fingers laced above his head, he stretched; his underarms were clean-shaven.

Wind tangled her hair and she lowered her eyes.

It was the wind, she supposed, that gave him a hard-on, thicker than a garden hose, but smaller than a cucumber. He caught her staring and blushed. A moment later, he spread his towel on the rocks and lay down, shielding his eyes with a white tube sock.

Think about something else, she told herself. Spreading her towel next to his, she mentally unfolded the travel brochures for Pergamom and Troy. At twelve, she'd wanted to be an archeologist; later, she planned to be a marine biologist. Now, thieves pillaged gravesites and dolphins choked on condoms. Even the beautiful ocean was doomed. Grains of sand—angular, sharp, and infinitesimal—filtered between her fingers. Before today, had she been feeling alive? Or dead?

At the smell of lighter fluid, she looked up. The sky behind Harun was postcard blue, the ochre cliff a backdrop for his face. God, to have such creamy skin. He shielded the tight, wound end of a joint with his cupped hand.

"My life after Army suck." He took a drag. "Sorry. Is only way I can make myself stand life now."

"May I?"

He plugged the joint between her lips. The dry sweet smoke seared her lungs. She coughed. Hadn't smoked in thirty years.

On the next exchange, her fingers slid against his hand. "Harun, Harun. Your name is a song."

Smoke rings spun toward her lips, and she inhaled his spent breath. A cottony taste thickened her tongue. The joint finished, she lay down again, cheek on her hands. Desire migrated to the hair follicles of her arm. She moved a fraction of an inch, then moved again.

"You bring water?" he said.

"No."

"Why not? American tourist always have water."

"I have a name, you know, and it's not 'American tourist'."

"Sorry, sorry, sorry."

For ten minutes they lay like parallel logs, and she thought she would die. He lit another joint. She pinned the roach with a hair clip.

"*Su*," he said. "Water in Turkish. I teach you Turkish word. You teach English."

"Your English is pretty good."

"Not good enough. If English good, I be night manager at Excelsior. You remember he? Short fat guy? He hate me. One night I want fuck Japanese lady, and I say him, 'Give me room key,' and he shout and say, 'No key!' and I say, 'Okay, I fuck she in hall.' On top floor is fold-up bed. I fuck she all night long. Next day manager make mouth like sour taste. What you think? His English good?"

She didn't remember the night manager's English, but she remembered the manager all right. He had picked up Bonnie's plate, trying to make her sit at the cruise ship's banquet table where widows had already taken out their grandchildren's pictures. Harun had swiped the plate out of the manager's hands and told Bonnie it was okay to sit at a table for two. A moment later, he presented her with a paper rose made from napkins and the offer of a private tour on his day off.

"Mrs. Bonnie," he said, "what means your name?"

"Beautiful."

"Beautiful," he said. "Is good."

"And it's not 'Mrs.' We say 'Miss' for unmarried women."

"Not marry?" He propped himself on his elbows. "But you beautiful womans. What's matter? You frigid?"

She laughed. "Not hardly. The right man never came along."

"Must be something wrong with American mans."

"The married men are okay. But in the single category you have the alcoholics, the Vietnam vets, the bitter divorced males, the sports junkies, the men who crash at nine o'clock, men with custody of small children and dogs, HIV-positives, ex-coke-addicts, AA groupies, tortured artists, and failed musicians, men who'll date for five years but won't get married, men who'll marry but screw your best friend, loners, workaholics, or impotent depressives. Oh, I forgot the men who only like thin women and only care about money."

Harun shook with laughter. "Mrs. Bonnie, too much words. Make money is business of man everywhere. Farm. Sell rug. Pick *oleeves*. But most important business is make jiggy jiggy. Hard work."

He flipped over onto his back, then to his front; over and back. Which side was up? Lying on her stomach, eyes closed, she wanted him desperately and hoped he was using these turns to close the gap. Her arm hairs felt skin. She raised her head. Only a wrinkle in her towel. Harun sat two feet away, examining his foot. Tears welled up in her eyes.

Smiling, he wiggled his toes. "You make *massaggi?*"

"You want a massage?"

"I want."

In an instant, she straddled his leg and pressed herself down against his thigh. Her knee spread his legs. The thin elastic of his underwear slid easily past the sharp bones of his hips, and as her fingers climbed the knobby bones of his spine, she adjusted her breathing to his. Then she turned and worked down his calf muscles to his feet. Finally, she put his big toe in her mouth and sucked it.

He turned over quickly and she gasped. "I don't do fronts."

"You know very well how to touch the body." He closed his eyes and she lay next to him, tucking herself in the crook of his arm. Maybe he would climb on top. The muscles of his stomach tightened. In the horseshoe of his ribs grew a thatch of hair and her fingers dove into it. He arched his back and moaned. Seizing her hair, he heaved her onto his stomach.

"You make saxophone?"

"What?" She raised her cheek from his belly button.

"You make saxophone?"

"No."

"Why not?"

"Because I want, I want..."

"What?"

"Never mind."

She was almost choking. She hated that gagging feeling.

He let go of her hair. "Thank you very much."

She waited to see if he would pull down her straps or slip his fingers inside her suit. He didn't move. She raised her cheek from his stomach and spat, then waded to the surf and washed her mouth out with the gritty backwash of the sea. There was a makeshift shower up by the car from which rusty water spurted. She swished handfuls and dressed.

By the time she returned he was fully clothed and skipping stones. He demanded that she swim, and she thought about lobbing rocks at him, but didn't, and stormed off down the beach. When she came back Harun avoided her eyes. Bonnie got in the car. The stench of cold tobacco was nauseating and grew more intense as Harun maneuvered up the switchbacks. Dust forced her to close the window. By the time the car reached the highway, she couldn't stop herself. "I make saxophone, and now you won't even look at me. What the fuck, Harun!" Just as he pulled onto the main road, an ancient tractor bore down on them. Harun turned to look at her and his eyes had a pained expression.

"Watch the road!" she screamed. He said nothing.

She endured the tightness in her chest until she finally saw her cruise ship rocking like a swan on the oily water, then let out her breath as he parked the car. The crenellated towers of an ancient caravansary blocked the view of Kucadasi's harbor but the smell of fishy water made brushing her teeth a priority. Before she could release herself from his tether, Harun took her elbow, steering past boys carrying trays with tiny glasses; she found herself inside a rug merchant's, plunked down on a bench, drinking apple tea. She swished the candy-apple liquid as if it were mouthwash.

So this was his game, a carpet commission. American tourist, American moneybags. Watching him scurry like a beetle on a pile of rugs that grew to be five feet high, she found it hard to contain her glee. "Gorgeous!" she clapped, eager to get back at him. The Garden of Eden carpets with animals were similar, but of lesser quality, to the three rolled up in her stateroom. After several apple teas, she had to find a bathroom. "Honestly, Harun, no more. They are gorgeous though."

Harun climbed off the pile, jingling the change in his pocket. "English always say, 'gorgeous, gorgeous' but never buy. Americans say 'no thanks' and always buy."

She laughed, thinking of the job of men—"farm, sell rug, pick *oleeves*, make jiggy jiggy." He was too much, this boy. She told the owner, a portly man standing by the door, that her credit card was maxed out; she had no intention of buying. Screaming Turkish insults at Harun, he cast them out, and she'd had enough revenge. They were now on a pedestrian mall. Past trinket-vendors' wooden carts, Bonnie saw her ship again and she unsnapped her purse. The day had been educational. Thanks.

Harun frowned. He wanted her to see his shop. Shop? She had supposed he was just some flunkie waiter. Before she could escape, he grabbed her elbow once again and herded her through more alleys. At an empty storefront squeezed between a bar and a vegetable vendor, parts of the gold letters of "Harun's Carpets" had been razor-bladed off. Paper and empty cardboard boxes were stacked against a padlocked door. What had happened to his business?

"Before Army. I borrow lots of money. But then I must go military. Two year in Army with Kurdish soldier. They not even speak my language, and I listen to them all night—talk, talk. When I come back, partner close store, take rugs to flat. Hard to sell. Now, men come mine house everyday. Say I no pay, bad thing happen."

"Why are you telling me?"

"No one else to tell." He clenched his fist and beat his chest. "I bring shame on family. Have pain in here so big, it knock hole."

She placed her fingers on his sleeve.

He flinched. "No touch. People see. Don't feel bad. Just Turkish way." He started off, hands thrust in his pockets. She caught up and told him, thanks, she was heading for the ship. But no. He was taking her to a pizza place. When she said she'd only go if he promised not to be in a bad mood, he said, "I feel how I feel. Is not same in America?"

Seated on the restaurant's terrace, she had to admit it was the most romantic place she'd been in years. It overlooked a deserted beach, and Harun blew smoke rings and watched the sky, where jets sliced arcs above distant islands. He said he thought it made no sense to disguise your feelings. She said it did. At least until you knew if a person could be trusted.

The pizza came and Harun spoke to the waiter. The lights dimmed. He clearly did not want to let her go, but why? The stomach knot, that usually came from wondering if a man thought she was too fat or needy, wasn't there at all. Couples on the ship ate like this, silent, content with each other's company. The sun floated on the indigo water, burning a molten hole in the horizon.

Finished, Harun ordered another drink and began to flick his lighter. She thought about asking him not to smoke, but decided against it. This was what married people did: put the other person's needs above their own. He banged the lighter on the table, flicking it again, then lobbed it over the balcony. "Shit lighter." He dipped his cigarette toward the candle; his features wavered behind the veil of heat.

"Shit life," he said.

She touched his wrist, and he let her fingers rest on his pulse. His eyes slid across the murky beach, stopping on the bay's far side. The Excelsior. Its windows, sunken ingots of gold, shimmered beneath the black water. She asked how much he made. A hundred a month, he said. Why'd she buy three carpets in Istanbul and not even one from him? "I didn't know I'd know you," she said.

He pursed his lips and stuck a napkin in the candle. It flamed up and he dropped the charred paper in his Orangina. "This winter I be cold. No money for winter clothes. No money give mine mother for food." He owed $562. The Turkish Mafia insisted on U.S. currency.

"Dollar like sultan," he said.

From her purse, she took $300 in bills and put them on the table. Harun sat up straight, scowling. He asked what it was for. His debt, Bonnie said. He held the bills to the candlelight. Counterfeit? When he tried to give the money back, she tucked it in his breast pocket, buttoning the tiny button.

In the parking lot, Harun put the key in the ignition and flung his arm over the seat behind her neck. A drunk ricocheted off the nearby restaurant wall.

"Like mine father," he said. "Many time, find him in street and carry home."
He dropped his head onto her shoulder, and she could not help but gather him
in her arms, smoothing his cheek with her knuckles. She dared not touch him
with her fingertips. That part of the day was over.

"You want?" he said.

"You don't have to."

"I do because I want."

At a neon-lit hotel near the railroad station, a clerk led them upstairs to a
room. Bonnie sat on a corner of the bed, pulling apart tufts on the spread
while Harun threw back the window's curtain. Beyond the broken glass was a
storage closet where steel chairs were stacked. Looking at their haphazard tilt,
Bonnie felt her chest tighten; warm prickles crept up her chin.

"My hotel better," he said. Of course, she thought, but she hadn't wanted
to go there. Harun took off his shoes and put them carefully on a tilted dresser
by the door. Stepping over her feet, he hung his shirt and undid his belt and
the top button of his pants. He turned on the TV to a soccer game. "Italy kill
us," he said.

Bonnie showered. When she opened the bathroom door, she saw Harun
sprawled on the bed, in pants and an undershirt, hands behind his head, his
ankle rotating with each kick on the screen. The loose forelock of his hair hung
down, and he brushed it back. Swaddled and damp, she climbed across his legs
and slid between the sheets. He reached for her breast. She squealed and pulled
the covers over her head. He folded them back. Hand behind her neck, he
kissed her so hard his gold necklace pressed into her clavicle. His eyes circled
her face. "Now, we get to know each other. Have all night."

Suddenly, he rolled off the bed. Back in fifteen minutes, he said. The room
door slammed. She lay very still, feeling the warp and weft of the linen. She'd
just about made up her mind to brave the streets alone when he returned with
a toothbrush, razor, and condoms. Thank God! She listened to him sing in the
shower—what a choir boy!—then a towel swished over the rack, and he stood
at the foot of the bed, arms and legs oiled.

She held out her arms. "Come here."

The mattress sagged.

Fingers working down his thighs, she told herself: go slow, go slow.

He wanted to look at her, and she tried to keep the covers up, apologizing
for her size.

"Not important to me. Tonight, we have little oasis, like middle of desert."
He threw the covers off the bed and held her knees apart as if climbing in a
canoe. Balanced between her thighs, scooping her hair away from her face, he
traced the outline of her lips.

"Darling, darling," he said. "My beautiful darling."

He tore open the wrapper of a condom with his teeth and slid it on expertly with his left hand. He lifted her leg onto his shoulder, and they began: part dream, part exercise.

In the middle of the night, he put his hand over her mouth. Outside the door, a man and woman argued. High heels clicked down the hall. "*Oroshpu!*" Harun whispered. "Not good hotel." He waited until it was quiet and rolled a joint; soon he was starving. He called down to the lobby. Someone brought up a tray piled with lamb kebabs and heaps of rice. Harun held a skewer to her lips and fed her the last grains with his fingers. Reveling in the steamy odor of garlic and spice, naked as an odalisque, she felt voluptuous and unashamed of her appetite.

"For strength. Important for Turkish man." He gathered up the plates and put the tray outside.

At five o'clock she'd had enough. Harun flopped over onto his side of the bed and pulled up a sheet. Was it good? he wondered. Yes, it was good, she said. He rolled himself into a cocoon, and she accidentally brushed his back. "Ohh," he moaned. "Turkish man say, smile on woman face, time to sleep. No more touch."

As Harun slept, Bonnie lay awake and imagined his face, beaming down at her. She envisioned them walking along the quay, holding hands. She felt young and beautiful and thin. Her fingers crawled up his neck and clutched the curls at the nape of his neck. He started to push her away, but changed his mind and laced his fingers through hers.

"They have good running shoes in America?" he asked.

They did.

"What best kind of jeans?"

"Shush, now," she said.

He kissed her fingers. "You know what I always dream of, darling?"

"No. What?"

"Cowboy boots." He pulled her hand across his body. "Size 33 European. American 10, I think." All but the top of his head was wrapped in sheets.

She jostled his shoulder, hesitated. She had to ask him. "Did you do this for money?"

"Why you say that?"

"Listen. Did you think, 'Poor Turkish boy fuck rich American lady. She give him presents!' Is that what was in your mind?"

His back went stiff, and he threw off her hand. Covering his head with the pillow, he said, "You see that on my face?"

"Your face?"

"Face not lie."

"Why no, I…"

She tugged on his pillow, but he rolled himself in a ball. Then he threw back the cover and stood naked beside the bed, pulling on his clothes.

"What are you doing?"

"Poor Turkish boy go to work."

"Oh please…what did I say? I'm sorry."

He sat down on the edge of the bed, putting on his shoes. One lace snapped. He held it up. "Cheap shit shoe. Poor Turkish boy no money for good pair."

Through the half-open bathroom door, she saw him dip his comb in water. Shaking, she picked up the sheet, wrapping it like a toga. He switched off the light. "Poor Turkish boy take back borrow car."

She fell on her knees and grabbed his cotton pants. "I said a stupid thing. It wasn't about you. It's about me."

He pulled her by the elbows, placing her like a naughty child on a corner of the bed. "Don't be a crier." Then he noticed the money in his pocket and threw it at her feet. Bills flew under the dresser. She fished one out. She hadn't meant to insult him; it was about her and her insecurities; the men at home were creeps; and she was fat, fat, fat. Why had he slept with her? That was all she wanted to know. He tried to open the door. She caught his belt and they wrestled until she pushed her whole weight against him and forced him against the dresser.

"*Oroshpu!*" he screamed, and she let go.

In the bathroom again, he looked over his shoulder at the mirror. "You make scratch in mine back. You fight like animal."

She sat down and bowed her head, clutching the edge of the mattress. "Please talk," she begged.

He whimpered like a child, before a sob tore from his throat. "I make for you my strong sex."

"But why?"

"Is not enough? You want more?"

"No. I'm exhausted."

"Then what you want?"

She waited. "Do you…love me…or at least care for me a little bit?"

He blew his nose, crying. "You not want me answer that." But she insisted.

"Okay," he finally said, "but after that, no more talk." Harun folded his handkerchief. "When we lay on beach, I think, 'Lonely woman. No sex in long time.'" He wanted to make her happy.

"And you did." She reached for him.

He jumped back. His eyes traveled across her breasts and face.

She turned away.

Finally, he said, "How…old you are?"

She looked down at the knotted laces of his shoes. "Fifty-five."

"Old as mine mother."

"Your mother?"

"She very beautiful when mine father carry her down from village. Now, she old Ottoman woman in head scarf. Go to bed at eight o'clock. She make best food for we. Always clean clothes. Every day white shirt. Good black sock. No hole. And shoes for school. I never barefoot. I never hungry."

He stared down, eyes glistening. From the adjacent room, water rushed up the pipes and hammered the walls. Harun turned and opened the door to the hallway.

"How will I get back to the ship?" she said.

"You rich American lady. Take taxi."

The latch clicked, and he was gone.

In the room, a steam bath from the night, a pocket of cold spread inward from the door. Bonnie felt the chill on her feet and looked down. The snapped shoelace. He would be crossing the lobby, the loose shoe rubbing his heel; he would pause and turn. He had to come back. She'd buy him anything he wanted. Anything.

Footsteps scraped on the stairs. Harun. She stooped to gather the money, then straightened up. No, let him pick it up.

The footsteps stopped and there were three hard knocks on the door. A gruff voice shouted. "*Bir fincan çay getirir misiniz?*" The knob turned and the door shook as if it might give way. Heart pounding, Bonnie took a quick step to brace the door with her shoulder. She clutched the knob in both hands.

Then it was quiet. In the hall a man sighed and began whistling. Dishes clattered on a tray. Whoever had delivered the food in the middle of the night had come to take it away. ∞

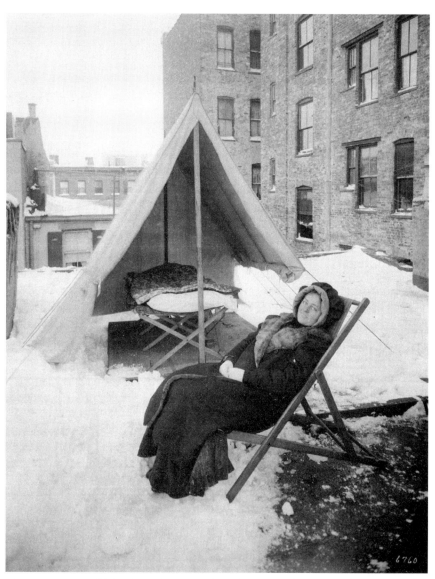

Home treatment of TB, circa 1909. Taking in the fresh air on the roof of a tenement. This treatment continued until the early 1950s, when the antibiotic isoniazid (INH) became available. Courtesy of Bellevue Hospital Archives: Chest Collection.

wifebeat

Michael Casey

OK this sergeant beats up his lady
we get the phone call to his house
on base housing
and bring him in
his company has to send
one very pissed off officer to sign
and then the subject wifebeater
must stay at his company's orderly room
for twenty-four hours before going back home
we get a frantic call from the company's CQ
that one particular sergeant has broken
this hour restriction and run off
of course we suspect his worst
the desk sergeant phone calls the guy's house
the guy answers
and the desk sergeant says
  is this sergeant wifebeater's house?
  is your wife home as we speak?
  sorry wrong number
and the MP's arrive just in time
the wife lets them in
and they find the sergeant hiding in the bathroom
sort of around the toilet
from the cruiser leaving his yard
the sergeant give his wife the finger
and that really teaches her something

&

Studies In The Subjunctive

Ruthann Robson

If I were to write you a letter on a card from a collection entitled "Autumn Leaves," this is what I would say: *Today is Anne Sexton's birthday*. Would you wonder how I knew? Would you remember, even in November, the calendar you gave me? She would have been 73 today. Or would not be. She could be dead of cancer (all those cigarettes! all that alcohol! her mother's painful extinction at 58). The subjunctive's sharp blade can cut in more ways than suicide.

If I try to imagine the knife, I cannot. It must have been steel and sharp, but was it serrated? It must have been accompanied by others, some smaller, some longer. How odd to feel the serious effects of an event for which I have no memory. Which is the purpose of anesthesia after all. The surgeon warned I might not survive. But after eight hours of cutting, I was still alive. The tumor was not.

Though all care be exercised, the letter could be fatal. Once my worry was that my card would contain some embarrassing grammatical error. Or at the most severe, that it would not arrive, having been trapped in the labyrinth of the postal service with no Ariadne to guide it to liberation. But now I imagine my creme-colored and rust-lined but still porous envelope nestled next to some cheaply porous envelope which just happens to be poisonous. It might be that I have sent spores to you when I meant to send a cheery greeting. Anthrax is now a part of our vocabulary.

Live life normally! The imperative from public officials. From my doctors. And so I try to continue my letter to you on Anne Sexton's birthday. Deciding to forgo her conditional age in favor of her unconditional poetry, I consult my bookshelves, brimming with what my mother once cursed as my vanity. My twenty-five-year-old paperbacks are infested with microscopic organisms: mold or even paper mites. I sneeze (could this be a symptom of something else?) as I look for an appropriate quote with which to begin. Something to serve as an epigraph. We are nothing if not literary; even our letters have inscriptions, like tombs. But my inspection of the book is distracted by underlining. In ink!

What a pompous college student I must have been. Thank goodness you didn't know me then. I often wondered whether, if my family had believed in poetry or the rules of grammar or that language could solve or soothe or be useful, I might have continued a career in literature. I might have not been so intimidated by the professors with their perfect accents and syntax. I might not have been mortified when I was directed to Fowler's A DICTIONARY OF MODERN ENGLISH USAGE *(and make sure you get the third edition)* after I handed in my paper on *The Uses of Ocean Metaphors in the Poetry of Anne Sexton.*

Now that the subjunctive is dying... This from the third edition, 1938. Anne Sexton would have been ten years old and my mother would have been one year old and the renowned H.W. Fowler would have been delighted about his work's immortality if he were still alive. *The subjunctive is, except in isolated uses, no longer alive.* Isolated in a suburban house seems better than being isolated in poverty. What if my mother had had the privilege of Anne Sexton? She probably still would have been depressed, but she would have been smarter about it. Or at least she could have driven a convertible bought by her father, the wool-factory owner, rather than walking to her job in the garment factory as a pregnant teenager.

Anne Sexton's psychiatrists thought it was only a matter of time. Isn't that what they always say, these doctors who chose the mind over getting their hands dirty? Before I found the surgeon who would agree to operate, other doctors recommended a psychiatrist who would assist me in accepting my death. I did not come from a family that believed that money should be wasted on a luxury like therapy. Wasn't that lucky?

In THE AWFUL ROWING TOWARDS GOD, this is what I have underlined: *wounding tides, the surf biting the shore, the sea that bangs in my throat, the sea without which there is no mother, the surf pushes their cries back.* There is the kind of reader who feels compelled to decorate her books with her own comments, little notes to the writer as if the author could read them, as if the author would be interested. I have not been her kind. But in this book, there exists one phrase of marginalia: *extended metaphor.* My handwriting is careful. Just as it must have been on my paper, *The Uses of Ocean Metaphors in the Poetry of Anne Sexton,* produced before the age of personal computers and at an age when I was too poor to purchase a typewriter. Somewhere in the universe, if only in the past, this paper still exists, echoing on the envelopes I would grace with my return address: *Ocean Avenue, North Sea Drive, Tidewater Lane, Shore Blvd.* Sexton's poem *At the Beach House* made me cry for what I did not have, would never have. Sexton's poem *Doctors (They are not Gods/though they would like to be),* I had ignored.

Today, at the inland post office, the postwoman comments on the beautiful calligraphy that graces my envelope, announcing my prosaic return address. Now that all mail is suspicious, that it could wind its way through the body in ways that could be incurable, I find her compliments comforting, talismanic. I would hope my doctors would be her kind.

Fowler classifies the uses of the subjunctive into four categories: alives, revivals, survivals, and arrivals. The alives consist of imperatives and conditionals in which no one could suspect the writer of *pedantry or artificiality.* (*I wish it were over* is the example provided by Fowler, the exemplar provided by Sexton, in life if not writing). The revivals are the province of poets and poetic writers, to be eschewed by the ordinary writer, who cannot but sound *antiquated* should he write *If ladies be but young and fair.* The survivals are not incorrect grammatically, but they *diffuse an atmosphere of dullness and formalism over the writing in which they occur.* Most objectionable, the arrivals are the best proof that the subjunctive should be put to rest: infected as it is with the illnesses of mixed mood, sequences of tenses, indirect questions, and the dangerous miscellaneous, risking pretentiousness. A risk Sexton avoided with her direct accessible language. Too direct, some critics declared.

If it were fall and it were 1974, Anne Sexton would be newly dead, and I'd be in college, and H.W. Fowler would still be dead, and I'd be drinking vodka in water glasses, and my mother would be threatening suicide, but my girlfriend would actually commit it. Not neatly in the garage, like Ms. Sexton in her cherished red car, but as colorfully daring as the dying leaves in New England. Blood splattered on the sidewalk in front of her house. In autumn, the sea doesn't dry up, but it might as well.

Were, in the subjunctive sense, is *applicable not to past facts, but to present or future non-facts* which belong to *utopia.* Fowler is quite precise on this. But to understand the exactitudes of grammar, one has to have an acquaintance with the basics. Before I went to school, the word *were* was a place of mystery to me, a utopian *where.* The past, present, and future were not tenses of verbs, but the captives of then, now, maybe someday. Listen to my mother talk: *We was going to get there then, but they was late and so we go nowhere.* No were.

Where you were that morning: in the CT machine at the cancer center; stopping for a bagel, cream cheese, no butter please; sleeping late with a former lover, sweaty with regrets that will soon dry small; on the plane you almost didn't make, feeling lucky to be going from Boston to L.A. for an interview; finishing the carpeting job in Queens before heading to the project downtown; at the Pentagon cookie shop, selling the last macadamia and chocolate chip; in the student lounge, looking up from the television set to see the same smoke, the same absence; at the veterinarian's office, picking up the dog's ashes; on the ledge, holding his hand, considering a choiceless choice; in the cockpit, between the sky and the ocean, aiming for the skyscraper's promise; on Chambers Street, using a briefcase as a shield; cradled in the stairwell, counting the flights, coughing and crying, dialing the cell phone, battery dead; in a place that will never be forgotten, never remembered, in heaven, in hell, in shock, in pieces, in tears, in a rage, incomprehensible, inarticulate.

Having revived.

Having arrived on the other side of some deep but invisible ocean, on the continent of those about whom the word *miracle* is whispered, I am still possessed of my Fowler's and my mother and my handwriting and my longing for a beach house.

Only now I don't understand suicide.

Only now I am suspicious of Anne Sexton (and the others, the others) for their deception: that death is romantic and not full of dullness and formalism; that death is literary and survivable.

Only now I wonder if Sexton (or Plath or Virginia Woolf...not to mention Hemingway) would have been diagnosed with a rare and almost always fatal cancer instead of depression; would she have fought her way into the clinical trials, past the doubting doctors, screaming *I am but young and fair*, too young to die, I am only 45, 30, 59, or 42 like me; or would she have succumbed, welcoming the morphine the doctors would provide in excess, as if they are gods and this is mercy.

If I were to continue my letter to you on Anne Sexton's birthday, inside the card with the images of the yellow gingko leaves and red maple leaves and the towering trees we once would have described as aflame but can no longer since we have seen what we have seen, I might still insist on trying to turn lines from Sexton into aphorisms with my careful inscriptions. *In November counting the stars/ gives you boils. Be careful of words/ even the miraculous ones. Many humans die./ They die like the tender, palpitating berries/ in November.* I would not write you how my abdomen still twists, a labyrinth constructed by my surgeon, my Ariadne, my rowing god with his oars of knives. Or of the dangerous miscellany of my side-effects, seeming to mimic the symptoms of anthrax poisoning, now that we know what the symptoms would be. I cannot but sound antiquated should I write: if oceans be but metaphors, then what is this salt that clings to my scars? And I would not but sound too much the poetic writer rather than the ordinary one, should I write you, my dear, that I struggle to get past the subjunctive (*what if? if not?*) every day, including this brilliant November day when the waves twist from a far off hurricane and we still strive in our boats hewn of grammar to arrive at utopia, or at least survive into some future. ✑

Dust and Oranges

Priscilla Atkins

The morning we linger over a linen breakfast,
blue reflections rippling through silverware,
the citrus trees' green fruit, strung like ornaments
around the perimeter,
studies sunlight, the way it cups
your snug mauve cap, licks hollow and cleft,
spills down your yellow sweater in buttery streaks.
I contemplate the history of gold, of dust.
You murmur: "No tubes.
Especially no feeding tube."
I long for courage, instinct, faith.
The air feels sepia. Grainy.
For a moment, two women
rendered in silence,
every spoon and saucer of breath
caught in separate exposures.
Each element deliberate, slow, essential.
Close up: orange peelings bloom
against China seas,
one hand gently moving towards another,
until they melt in a ship's wake, like winter roses.

∞

Mock Orange

Linda Goodman Robiner

My mother comes in the front door.
That smell is too much, she says, nodding
toward the mock orange.
Those little white flowers are pretty,
but the bush smells too ripe, don't you think?
Maybe you should cut it back.
It smells like those locust trees in New York
near the hospital—so sweet
they'd take over your senses, cross the line.

I tell her I dreamed of Jeff last night.
I don't like to think about dreams.
I push them away, try to forget everything bad
like when Jeff insisted on telling me about...you know.
She looks out the window.
I told him I knew but didn't want to know.
I didn't want my friends to feel sorry for me.
I went to the beauty shop when he was sick
and played bridge with my ladies.
And honey, when you write poems about him,
you don't say what he died of, do you?

&

Going South

Natalie Pearson

My mother is in a hurry, but I'm not sure where she wants to go.

She sits up, excitedly, in the second-hand wheelchair, its armrests newly patched with packing tape, propelling herself with her good foot toward the farmhouse door. "Dammit," she says, as her bad foot gets hung up on the ancient stove. "I want to go," she says, ramming the sagging footrest against the oven door. "I want to go…" but the word she wants won't come. She is halted here, aphasia trapping her words as surely as she herself is caught in this dingy, crumb-spattered kitchen.

Pausing, she starts over.

"There's a building," she says. "Down there, you know." She searches my face, willing me to understand. "The most beautiful one I ever saw. I want to see it. I want to go. Now."

"A building?" I ask, confused. I doubt mostly because I know her, know that only a blessed obliviousness to buildings has allowed her to live happily here in this sagging, neglected farmhouse with its peeling paint and smelly corners.

"What kind of building?" I ask, though she probably can't say. At 84, Mom has spent the last eight years hobbled by brain surgery that left her unable to speak clearly, walk, or use her right hand. The aphasia, though, is the worst. Words balk, hide, refuse to come entirely.

"I don't know—there's a big sign," she says pointing off, away from the farmhouse. "You go south."

I hesitate, afraid to go out alone with her, without help to lift her in and out of the car. What would happen if she needed, suddenly, to go to the bathroom, as she often does? The farmhouse is isolated. I don't know these back roads well and can't say where we'd end up.

"I need to go to the store anyway," Mom says then, and I can tell she is grasping. "We need things."

"No, we don't," interjects Louie, my stepfather, who had appeared to be napping in his naugahyde chair. "What are you going to buy at the store?" Louie asks, angrily. "There's nothing we need."

As Louie sees it, people think they need altogether too much these days, and he's determined to need almost nothing. Louie takes care of Mom, an exhausting job he does with mostly gruff adequacy. Ever since he brought her home from the nursing home where she was parked for a year after the second, debilitating brain surgery, Louie has insisted on going without. The nursing home cost too much, he insisted. They overfed Mom, babied her. She got soft and lazy there; he was sure of it.

Softness disgusts Louie more than anything else about the world today. It's why he won't have air-conditioning in the pickup, and chafes when we bring electric fans to cool the farmhouse. It's why he still farms at 89, an age when virtually all his peers have moved on, either to town or to the graveyard. It's why he does it organically—no shortcuts, none of what he calls "clowned" or "harmoned" cattle, no genetically modified soybeans or Roundup Ready corn. Mom has always been right there with him, too—buying only second hand clothes, diluting generic dish soap to stretch it just a little further, refusing to move into the modern house on the farmstead that Louie rents out. He didn't like the idea of moving, she explained, "and besides, it's too fancy for me."

But all of Louie's cut corners have stranded her here. She needs a softer view now, and I know it has to come from me.

"It's fine," I say. "We don't have to go to the store. We'll just see what we can see. It isn't a big deal."

However dubious I am about our destination, it can't outweigh the fact that I feel like a really bad daughter most of the time now. I can't protect her against age and illness. I can't heal her wounded brain, fend off her doctors, soften her husband. Instead, I make amends with small gifts—a loaf of crusty bread, a Louie Prima CD, lilacs in a mason jar. This little drive to nowhere would be just such a gift.

I struggle to get Mom out the door with its cracked glass and broken hinge. Louie, after a short inner scuffle between his anger and his innate need to be helpful, follows us down the disintegrating sidewalk, through the sagging gate, and then—without meeting my eyes—easily lifts Mom out of the wheelchair and into the too-low front seat of my car. Once she is buckled in, the chair stowed in the trunk, she and I head out the driveway. Knowing that Mom wants me to follow her directions, we veer left and head south over southern Iowa hills so green I find myself thinking of Ireland.

All that gentle beauty calms me, helps fade the picture in my head of my stepfather's angry face as he watched us drive away. There was a time when I found Louie admirable, thought his stubborn dedication to hard work and doing things the old way charmingly idiosyncratic. Though conversation with Louie has always been impossible, I liked his wiry strength, his fierce blue eyes. He resembled those smart, extra healthy charolet cattle of his who were perpetually escaping through the sloppily patched fences. But that was back in the days when Mom cooked, cleaned, and tended their old farmhouse, back when she could get herself to the bathroom, when she could still charm him into regularly using a washrag (Louie doesn't bathe) and occasionally applying deodorant before they headed out on their round of dances and political meetings. Louie has long supported both the NRA and the Sierra Club, listened religiously to Paul Harvey, and steered all conversations to the mysterious—but to him undeniable—connection between failing public schools, use of farm chemicals, and modern parents who won't spank their children. Back then, Mom could still argue him out of his most ridiculous ideological stands or happily cancel his vote when he failed to budge.

Louie is Mom's third husband, and she married him 18 years ago with few expectations. On most important things, they were of one mind. It was essential, they agreed, to dance several times a week, to keep busy with meetings, gardening, and politics; their relationship was built on that agreement. I liked Louie back then, back before Mom grew suddenly, devastatingly, old and sick. Back when she still had the power to leaven his harshness. Back before she became a hostage to his rigid view of the world.

Most people think of time as a mellowing force, but I know it is no such thing. Watching my mother and Louie steep together in the brine of advanced age, I know that growing old distills some people into their most distinct and rigid qualities. Thrift cooks down to obsessive cheapness, vanity curdles into hypercriticalism, and a once admirably willful person turns nearly to stone with stubbornness. In Louie's case, his three essential elements—frugality, stubbornness, and resistance to change—have simmered together. The resulting stew means that nothing gets fixed, bought, or altered if Louie has anything to say about it. At the farmhouse, where he has lived all his life, broken windows don't get repaired, cracked plates remain in the cupboard. If the milk goes sour, you drink it down without a flinch. For him it is a matter of principle—not necessity, as most people understand it. Louie has money in the bank, a fair amount of it, I suspect, though he refuses to fill out any of the financial forms required for government insurance programs.

"Nobody in the government needs to know how much I got," he insists, impervious to our arguments about practicality, entitlement, procedure.

Money is the reason Louie stopped giving Mom her pills—the small white ones for blood pressure and the capsules to prevent seizures. They cost too much, Louie said, and they made her "owly." At first the lapsed prescriptions infuriated me, but she has gotten along fine without them for more than a year. Her blood pressure is perfect. Seizures come and go, exactly as they did when she was medicated to prevent them. I suspect money is also the reason Louie refuses to consider moving to town, to a place that would accommodate Mom's wheelchair, with reliable heat and a sewer that isn't backing up all the time, where they could take advantage of congregate meals, and home health services. None of that is for Louie and is thus not available to Mom. I have consulted lawyers, social workers, Mom's family doctor. They all say the same thing: as Mom's husband, Louie calls the shots. Unless we can prove that he isn't feeding her, or find signs of physical abuse, he is in charge.

"I have to put up with it, with him," Mom says to me on the phone, after an especially bad day. At this late stage, I can't tell her any different. It is the deal she has struck, the contract she signed with each of her husbands, of whom Louie is unquestionably the best: marriage obviates dissent. When you tie yourself to a man, you tie your own hands. I don't agree, but now is not the time to argue.

Wifely dependence is ugly and out of fashion, a yoke I don't have to wear. And yet for Mom, independence was ugly, too. In her life, being alone meant raising five kids without help or support, spending days cleaning hospital rooms and tending to other women's laundry and children, then returning home to kill chickens and weed a garden so we had enough to eat. Marriage freed her from that struggle, and until recently I could hardly argue that it wasn't a bargain.

And so on this day—the day Mom wants to go for a ride—I know that this is one thing, one small escape, I can offer.

So we get in the car and drive south. South past the sanitation company, south past the dirt race track, south past a fallen down farm complex, and suddenly the view is so simple and so lovely we both gasp.

"It is pretty back here," I say.

"Yes, it is. It, it…it's *old*." That last word spilled off her tongue in a way that tells me it isn't the word she wanted or the one she meant. Like so many of her words these days, it is simply the one that comes out.

"I don't see any beautiful buildings out here, though."

"No. Me neither. Maybe I was wrong about the direction. I'm not too, too…you know. I'm not too smart these days."

And again she searches my face, willing me to understand.

"Mom, you are one of the smartest people I know," I say. "And it doesn't matter, finding the building."

"No, you're right," Mom says, leaning back. "All I wanted was a ride." ∞

Developmental Psychology

Meghan Hickey

for my mother

Cat tips cup to lap
the water, dribble on

her chin, and crow drops
pebbles in a glass

to solve his thirst.
A stranger once poured me

this riddle: which
holds more, this cylinder

or that? Drops fell
as she transferred the water

to the fatter, squatter
from the leaner, longer

cup. I pointed
to the latter. Stranger

scribbled in her book.
"No, no,"

she saccharined, "there is
the same in both,"

then pulled
a pink stuffed kitten

from her purse. A base
reward: how could

Interrogator know
I took as evidence

the blotter's damp
and spreading stain, that is

the fallen drops, i.e.
her pouring lack? And in

our kitchen! Well
she could have asked

how many stripes on tabby
cats; I would have answered

—cinch. It was
a schoolday; I

had work to do
(a spelling bee

tomorrow and
addition). As I sat

I knew the daylight
savings wasted.

     ❧

Children with TB on the Southfield Ferry, Dec. 20, 1910, being taught by Miss Spence (later a founder of the Spence-Chapin School). Photographer: Jessie Tarbox Beals. Courtesy of Bellevue Hospital Archives: Chest Collection.

Home Free

Daniel C. Bryant

Quickly it came squirting out in his hand. Tom held onto the side of the basin as his knees buckled slightly. A minute later he pulled up his jeans and washed up. He wiped off the rim of the toilet bowl carefully with Kleenex and flushed.

He tiptoed into the living room and stood beside the coffee table. He stretched his arms over his head, nearly reaching the ceiling light, touched the toes of his slippers, spread his legs to the side as far as he could, and leaned out over first one knee, then the other. After a few pushups he rolled over onto his back on the rug. He looked up at the ceiling, then reached over to the coffee table for his clipboard. He scribbled "voice-over" next to the dialogue on the top sheet, then crossed it out and fell asleep.

Hen was crying. Tom got up slowly from the floor and went to the crib in the far corner of the bedroom. He peered over the crib side at the little boy tangled in the sheet.

"Hey, my man," he said, "what's happening? I bet I know what's happening. My man is soaking wet is what's happening, am I right?"

The boy stopped crying at the voice and at the feel of Tom's index finger probing the wet Pamper. Tom picked him up and carried him at arm's length into the bathroom. He stood Hen on the wash stand, broke the tabs, worked the Pamper out from between the boy's legs, and dropped the soggy mass into a plastic Shop 'n' Save bag. Then he washed the boy with warm, soapy water, patted him dry, dusted him with powder, and put on a fresh Pamper. As he worked, Tom explained how it was time Hen, being nearly three, should be doing some serious thinking about the wetting. So they'd have more time for things other than changing diapers, Tom said. Fun things.

A little after six, after Hen had eaten his grilled cheese, Tom was watching the local news and turning the pages of the big Richard Scarry truck and train book for Hen who was seated on his lap. Hen was not looking at the book. He was looking at the news, too. The phone rang in the kitchen.

"Mommy!" Tom said as he sat Hen down beside him on the couch. "Pad Thai, what do you think?"

Hen smiled.

Tom went into the kitchen to answer the phone, talked briefly, and returned to the couch.

"Was I right or was I right?" he said, leaning over to feel Hen's Pamper. "Way to go, my man. Pee-pee time." He picked up the boy and carried him slung over his shoulder into the bathroom. He detached the Pamper and set him on the toilet. Tom waited, looking away.

Nothing happened.

"Got to be pee-pee, Hen," Tom said. "There's always pee-pee. Got to try, my man, got to push push push like this. Watch Daddy." And Tom bore down, grimacing, until his face bloated red.

Hen watched. He made a face back. But there was no urine.

"Okay, my man," Tom said, "you tried and I'm giving you full credit for that, but where that pee-pee's hiding you got me."

Tom carried the boy back into the living room where Wheel of Fortune glowed on the television screen. They sat on the couch watching, Hen on Tom's lap again, sucking his thumb. "B" lit up on the board. Tom pronounced it with such a sudden burst that Hen's thumb was jerked from his mouth. "Like this: B. B. Buh. Boy. Big Boy. You say it. Please."

Hen said nothing.

At the jingle of keys Tom and Hen turned as one toward the front door.

"Mommy's home!" Ann called out musically as she entered. Tom greeted her with a kiss and brought the take-out sack into the kitchen while Ann carried Hen into the bedroom, talking and hugging him all the way. Tom hung up her white jacket that was weighted with stethoscope and index cards, and returned to the couch. He hit *mute* and scanned back and forth through the channels. As he did so he could hear Ann reading what sounded like one of the Pooh stories to Hen, then kissing him good night.

They ate at the coffee table by candlelight.

"Anything today?" Ann said.

"He's got DaDa down pat, that's for sure."

"Well, not to worry, they say."

"Till three." Tom chewed another mouthful of noodles and went on, still chewing, "I'm not worried though, not really."

"He'll pick up on it," Ann said.

"Hmm. They do, they say. Pick up on stuff. So tell me, who'd you cure?"

"Put in a subclavian. On my own; Smitty wasn't even in the Unit. And got this AIDS case? Won't take his damn cocktail. Sits there. Shade down. You know...*dying*."

"How stupid is that?" Tom said. Ann slowly shook her head.

After they had cleaned up from supper, Tom and Ann lay side-by-side on the couch and watched CNN for a while. They went in to check on Hen who was wet but didn't wake when Ann changed him. They got ready for bed and eased under the covers with hardly a sound.

"There's medicine," Ann whispered.

"For?" Tom whispered back.

"Wetting."

"Now you're worried?"

"Not worried. I'm just saying."

"If he'd just stop wetting and start talking we'd be golden."

"We're pretty golden as it is," Ann said, brushing Tom's ear with her lips. "Don't you think?"

They made love quickly and quietly in the dark.

Tom was sitting on one of the benches, his clipboard on his lap. From time to time he looked up from his writing to watch Hen who was sitting cross-legged on the ground next to the low end of the kiddy slide. Hen was picking up colored bits of Styrofoam mulch that covered the central play area, placing them in piles, more or less by color, on the end of the slide. A little girl in a soiled jumper skipped over to watch him work, one sandal strap flapping. After a few minutes of study, she brushed all his piles off the end of the slide, went around to the ladder, climbed up, and slid down. Hen watched without saying a word. He made a face, to no one, then started back in with the bits.

A heavy-set young woman in tight slacks and tank top walked over from the bench where she had been sitting and jerked the little girl off the ground by one arm. "Ruthie!" she shouted. "Where's your manners? Don't ever let me see you...." She dropped the girl and detoured back close by Tom.

"Sorry 'bout that. He yours?" she asked.

"Yeah. No problem."

"Kids," she said, shaking her head. "Who needs 'em?"

He watched the woman return to her bench and sit down. She stuffed the front of her tank top, which had ridden up over the bulge of her lower abdomen, into her slacks and picked up a magazine. At that distance, he couldn't see which magazine it was. The little girl was now halfway up the slide ladder again. She stopped there and leaned out to peer sideways at the woman. The woman looked up and scowled, at which point the girl stuck out her tongue, clambered back down, and skipped over to the swings. The woman looked at Tom, contorting her mouth and raising her eyebrows, and shrugged. Tom looked at the words he'd written on the sheet of paper on his clipboard.

Ann was on first-call at the hospital. Tom had Grape Nuts with banana for dinner while Hen ate fish sticks, dipping each one meticulously into a large bowl of ketchup. After supper they watched Wheel. Tom read Hen two books, including all the noises. He changed the diaper, wet again, before putting him down.

"You know, my man," Tom said as he did so, "it's okay to be wet overnight because that's a really long time overnight, like ten hours. But when you're awake and you can feel what's going on down there and could, you know, do something about it, it's not really okay. Know what I'm saying? Anyway, I've been thinking. And what I've been thinking is starting tomorrow you and me we're going to have this schedule like every maybe two hours? On the potty. To be sure." Tom paused. "No pressure. Everything's cool. Just to be sure. About the pee-pee. Deal?"

He lay the boy down on his back in the crib and pulled the blanket to his chin.

"See you tomorrow, buddy. Sweet dreams. I'll leave the hall light on okay?" And he leaned way over the railing to kiss the boy on the forehead.

Tom went into the kitchen to put dirty clothes into the laundry bag by the door. Then he went into the living room and sat down on the couch. He picked up his clipboard and read through the top pages, making notes in pencil as he went. He inserted a fresh sheet under the clip, squared it up, and wrote a few words before stopping and frowning up at the ceiling. A few minutes later, he picked up the remote. He lay back and ran the muted channels.

Two women were sitting on one of the benches at the playground when Tom and Hen arrived. Three boys were struggling to get a rock nearly the size of a bowling ball up the incline of the big slide. They stopped from time to time to argue over the best way to do that. Tom took Hen down the kiddy slide on his lap a few times, then left him at his station at the bottom. Just as Tom was sitting down on his usual bench, the heavyset woman entered the playground with Ruthie. The little girl ran directly to the big slide to watch the boys who were already half way up. Rather than sit down herself, the woman looked at Tom for a minute, looked back at Ruthie and shouted to her, "I'm watching!" She walked to Tom's bench, glanced at Hen, then looked back at Tom.

"Cute," she said, thumbing in Hen's direction.

Tom looked up. He made a humming sound in his throat. The woman sat down next to him on the bench. "Mind?" she said. Then, leaning toward him, "I know I'm kinda big but…."

"Fine," Tom said, looking over at Hen who had stood up and was now walking toward the big slide. The boys had worked the rock clear to the top where Ruthie had joined them. "Hen!" he called, "Where you going?" At the sound of the voice, Hen sat down in the open space right where he was. He began picking up colored bits and stuffing them into the sides of his moccasins.

"Cute," the woman said again. "What're you doing?" she asked a moment later, pointing to Tom's clipboard. "You don't mind my asking."

"Nothing," Tom said.

"Looks like you're taking notes or something. On your kid. I'm not crowding you am I?"

"No, really."

"Glandular's what they say. I'm thinking of going to the clinic for tests and stuff. What Ruthie's dad always said. But I don't know what do you do for glands if you got 'em anyway, huh? Ruthie!"

The boys had released the rock which careened down the slide and landed in an explosion of colors, and now they and Ruthie were sliding down after it en masse. When they hit the ground, the little girl looked over at the woman. Hearing nothing further, she hopped up, brushed off, and walked to where Hen was sitting by himself.

"It's a screenplay," Tom said. "I'm writing a screenplay."

The woman turned back to him, wrinkling her nose as she did. "Like shows and stuff?" she said.

Tom made the humming sound again.

"You know what's really great?" she said, rubbing her hands together and squinting as she addressed him. "Prison movies. Like that guy what's his name with the bird and the little wagons like? Escapes and stuff 'cause you always want 'em to make it no matter what they did. That what your show's about? Something like that?"

"Something like that. A robbery in LA. Beverly Hills actually. Which you're not sure of till the end, whether it's all part of a movie-within-a movie or not. Kinda complicated."

"Wow," the woman said. "You been out there?"

"Lived there all my life," Tom said. "Up till July, that is."

"Wow. You must be famous."

"Hey, I wish." He stood up. Ruthie was handing colored bits to Hen now, which he was putting in his mouth. Tom walked over to him and made him spit them out. He picked Hen up and settled him into the stroller.

"See ya," the woman called from the bench as they began to leave.

"Yeah," Tom answered over his shoulder. "See ya around."

Ann was exhausted from her night on call. She read *Frog and Toad Are Friends* to Hen while Tom cooked a mushroom omelet. At the table, between bites, Ann highlighted a photocopied article she had brought home with her.

"I've got a good feeling about our schedule," Tom said. "Of course nothing has happened so far but I really think he's getting the idea. What's expected. You think?"

Ann turned the page.

"About the schedule working, Ann, do you think it's too much, I don't know, regimentation?"

"Regimentation?" Ann said, looking up.

"Yeah. At his age, I mean."

"I'm sorry, I…."

"No, I shouldn't be disturbing you." He speared a mushroom with his fork. "And talking's the thing anyway. And we have till three on that."

"Churchill was four they said. Remember? I think it was Churchill."

Tom cleaned up the dishes as Ann got ready for bed.

"I'm really sorry, Tom," she whispered when he sat down on the side of the bed next to her. "I didn't close my eyes once last night and that kid with cerebral edema? Dead, no post. And I had to tell the mother. Good learning experience, Smitty said. You should've seen the woman though, Tom, I mean…."

Tom leaned over and kissed her on the temple. He stroked her long blond hair, sweeping stray filaments into silky arcs behind her ear. But she was already asleep. As he tiptoed from the room, he checked Hen curled next to the bars of his crib, then went into the kitchen and microwaved his mug of coffee left from the morning. He took it into the living room and sat down on the couch with his clipboard. He wrote a full page quickly, reread it, and crumpled it methodically, quietly, into a ball. He turned on the television low, and watched.

Because it was drizzling, Tom dressed Hen in his rain pants, slicker, and rain hat, and brought the umbrella with them to the playground. When they arrived, Ruthie was sitting on the top step of the big slide, looking straight up as she held on. The woman was sitting on a bench wearing a sweatshirt and shorts this time. They were the only ones at the playground and neither one had rain gear. Tom settled Hen under the big slide where it still looked to be dry, and went over to sit on the bench next to the woman.

"How 'bout this?" she said, as if talking to herself. "You'd have to have some kind of outside help but they shoot these smoke bombs. Over the wall into that, you know, place where they exercise? Only, one's got a gun in it and maybe disguises or saws or something and in the, you know, confusion and smoke, the guy gets the stuff." She finally turned to him. "What do you think?"

"Pretty good. Only I think those areas probably have screens over the top. For that very reason."

"Just an idea. Use it if you want."

Ruthie started crying. She was stuck on the damp metal of the slide partway down. At the sound overhead, Hen crawled out and peered up at her. He threw some of his colored bits at her. She picked off a few that had stuck near her and threw them back, giggling through her tears.

It started to rain in earnest. Tom put up his umbrella and handed it to the woman.

"Ruthie!" she called. "Get down off there. Can't ya see it's raining? We got to go." She stood, holding out the umbrella toward Tom and said, "You guys want to come? We're just over there."

Tom put Hen in the stroller and they followed Ruthie and the woman out of the playground. Less than two blocks away the woman led them through a chain link gate, up a cement walk to a low blue duplex. The woman left the umbrella dripping in the entryway and they all went into a large living room furnished only with a couch, a La-Z-Boy, a small refrigerator, and a widescreen television sitting on the bare floor. The television was on, muted.

"Not much going for it except dry, huh?" the woman said, holding out her arms. She turned on the sound and Hen and Ruthie sat down in unison in front of the set. The woman flopped onto the couch and Tom sat down next to her, on a blanket and sheet that were covering his end. They all watched the screen which showed a hospital room. A nurse was choking back tears as she adjusted an IV bottle.

Tom leaned back, sighing as he did so. The woman turned toward him at the sound, her full cheeks slowly dimpling with a smile. He reached over and began pulling up her damp sweatshirt. She started to help, awkwardly, then stood and led him through a doorway into a tiny bedroom. Nailed to the wall over a narrow bed was a Springsteen poster. She closed the door. They took off their own clothes. The woman handed Tom a condom from a low bedside chest, then lay down on her back on the bed. Tom climbed up on top of her. As he rolled the condom on, he stared down at the round contours of her face, her wide-open gray eyes. And, still staring, he began to root and work back and forth until with a muffled groan and whimper he collapsed upon her.

"'It's okay, hon," she said, patting him on the back of the head. "It's okay."

He slept deeply, but not long. As soon as he awoke he got up, pulled on his clothes, and went out into the living room.

"C'mon my man," he said to Hen, still in front of the television. "Got to go." Then he called out, "Hey, using the facilities okay?" He led Hen into the bathroom, pulled down the rain pants and Pampers, and set him still in his slicker and rain hat on the toilet. "C'mon, pee-pee. Schedule time." In a few seconds he heard the sound of water tinkling in the bowl. "Hen, way to go! We did it! Yeah, pee-pee!" He sealed the Pamper back on, and carried Hen out into the living room in the crook of his arm.

"See ya, mister famous man," the woman called from the bedroom.

Tom put Hen down and walked to the bedroom door. She was still lying there on her back on the narrow bed, large and naked and pale.

"I don't know," he said softly. "I don't know what to say."

Hen was already in bed. Ann made a stir-fry and served it with green tea. She lit an almond-colored spherical candle. The scent of bay leaves filled the living room.

"To mark the occasion," Ann said.

"I'll drink to that," Tom said, raising his cup.

"Now if he'd just talk we'd be home free."

"Right," Tom said. "I can't wait. Good title, too."

"Title?"

"Home Free."

"For?"

"Oh, nothing. Idea I had."

Ann put down her chop sticks to give him her full attention.

"Idea for an idea more like," he said. "You know. Don't want to jinx it."

"*Comme tu veux,*" Ann said.

They ate in silence for a few minutes, then Ann put her chop sticks down again. "You know this weekend?" she said. "I'm off starting Friday. After clinic. How about we take Hen up the coast overnight? Some B & B like Camden maybe."

"Or maybe Thomaston. I hear it's got the Maine state prison."

"Seriously, Tom. Be kinda fun wouldn't it? To poke around?"

"It would, Ann, it really would."

"I'll ask around tomorrow and we can call—might need reservations. Smitty'll know places."

Tom sipped his tea. He looked at Ann over the top of his cup. "Wonder what he'll say."

"He knows everything, that guy. Amazing."

"No," Tom said. "Hen. What Hen will say. First. When he talks. His first words. Of his whole life."

Ann watched her husband as he explained his meaning. And into the silence that followed. ☙

Differential Diagnosis

David Milofsky

Although Sylvia had been drawn to medicine by a desire to help people, her choice of specialty had been less altruistic, since a great many patients whom she saw could not be helped, nor even nurtured in a productive way. What had attracted her to neurology was what she perceived as the elegance of the primary diagnostic tool of that specialty, the neurological examination. If someone came to see a gastroenterologist or a cardiologist with pain, the physician generally would locate the cause and proceed to treat it if she could. With neurology, things were seldom so simple. Medicine was often called an art rather than a science, but it was never so true as in neurology. Diagnosis required patience, judgment, subtlety, and time, qualities Sylvia felt were lacking in her personal life, which was more often scattered, hurried, and chaotic.

Yet sitting in her white lab coat with a patient's medical history spread out before her on the table, Sylvia felt cool, removed, in control, though obviously it was someone else's world she was controlling and even that was often a necessary illusion. Sylvia could almost never really control anything; she could only describe it, or perhaps treat it, which was seldom easy. Of course, the middle-aged woman who had come in that morning complaining of undifferentiated spells of dizziness would undoubtedly have felt differently about the current course of her life.

Even the fact that Sylvia was seeing the woman was significant, since these days family practitioners were generally reluctant to refer patients to specialists unless it was absolutely necessary. In medical argot these doctors were referred to as "gatekeepers" and received a certain sum from managed care companies to allot annually for referrals. In practical terms, every time a primary care doctor sent one of his patients to a specialist, it meant money out of his or her pocket and scrutiny by the insurance case managers. As in most things regarding the new regime, there was some logic to this practice, for in most cases a sore throat would be only a sore throat and there was no need for a more thorough examination. But there were cases of head and neck cancer that might be missed and, in any case, there were financial incentives for the primary care doctors to go with the percentages. It was good finance but not always good medicine.

In this instance, Sylvia knew the primary care physician only slightly, and the scribbled note on the chart alluding to "Poss. syncope or ataxia," was of little help since it could mean almost anything or nothing at all. The most important tool a neurologist could have when seeing a patient for the first time was a good referral and Sylvia didn't have this, no doubt because the primary care doctor didn't have time for such things. With the advent of managed care, doctors complained about many things: reduced income, oversight by ignorant case managers, demanding patients holding computer-generated printouts about their illnesses. But the real loss was time—time to listen, time to care who the patient was and what might be troubling her. And while Sylvia knew this shouldn't matter, that they should all make the time—regardless of their personal problems—doctors were human and since they seldom knew their patients, there was less of a personal investment in the individual. That had been lost, replaced by distrust and cynicism on both sides. The patients were more litigious and the doctors spent more time doing unnecessary tests to cover themselves. Nobody really found this rewarding, but it was the current reality they all lived with, and Sylvia knew it was likely to get worse.

So today she would have to start from the beginning, something that always annoyed patients who felt they had told the same story to several different doctors, and often enough they had. Still, the differential diagnosis for dizziness—the list of things that could be causing it—was vast. Even the term dizziness was only a vague abstraction, meaning different things to different people. Sylvia took a deep breath and went next door to the examining room.

The examining room was small and painted a light blue that mimicked the patient's complexion. The patient was thin, with a narrow face and beady gray eyes, but her curly brown hair made her seem somehow soft. Her husband sat next to her on a stool too small for his bulk. Both had pinched expressions and the room smelled vaguely of sweat and after-shave. Sylvia understood. No one looked forward to coming to a specialist and no matter what the symptoms were, everyone's first thought was cancer. She smiled in what she hoped was a reassuring way, and extended her hand. "Mrs. Simmons, I'm Dr. Rose. It's nice to meet you." She nodded at the husband.

Mrs. Simmons swallowed air but said nothing, as if she were unable to speak. Sylvia was used to patients being nervous; neurology was a daunting specialty known to the general public, if it was known at all, for the celebrity dinners held to raise money for incurable diseases with unpronounceable names. Sylvia sat in a chair and fixed her gaze on her patient, blocking out all other thoughts. "Mrs. Simmons, Dr. Peters sent you to see me because you've been experiencing some symptoms, but I want you to understand that just being here doesn't constitute a diagnosis. Right now, we just have some symptoms."

"You mean she isn't sick?" the husband asked hopefully.

Sylvia turned to the man and smiled again. "I don't know if she's sick or not, Mr. Simmons. I just met your wife. That's what we're here to find out. I want to take a history and examine her. But that's just a start."

"She's not right," the man said. "I'll tell you that right now. Not how she always was. She fell down the other morning and practically dropped a frying pan on the baby."

Sylvia nodded. "That's not normal. What I meant was that sometimes people have transient episodes, which have no cause, or none we can find. And that sometimes don't recur. We call those attacks idiopathic."

The word impressed the Simmonses, which gave Sylvia a chance to turn her attention back to the woman. The husband wasn't her patient and regardless of his relationship with his wife, he couldn't really tell Sylvia how she felt, only his impression of his wife's infirmity. "Mrs. Simmons, Dr. Peters said you've been having problems with dizziness at home. Could you tell me exactly what you mean by that?"

Mrs. Simmons looked perplexed by Sylvia's question, as if it were too obvious. But patients used dizziness to describe a variety of sensations, including light-headedness, faintness, a spinning sensation, mental confusion, headaches, blurred vision, and tingling in the arms or legs, all of which might indicate various diseases, anxiety, eyestrain, or nothing. In fact, in Sylvia's experience it was usually nothing identifiable. "Doctor, I'm dizzy," was almost useless in a clinical sense but Sylvia had to start somewhere.

Mrs. Simmons' face was screwed up in concentration. "It's like, all of a sudden my feet aren't there," she said.

Gait disturbances, Sylvia thought, and remembered Peters' note about ataxia. The differential on that ran a half-page in Harrison's *Textbook of Internal Medicine*. "Do you mean you can't feel your feet? That they're numb? Or do you have difficulty walking, maintaining your balance when you go outside?"

The question was frustrating for the woman because it was clear that in her terror, Mrs. Simmons hadn't been able to consider her condition analytically or describe it very well. Now, suddenly, subtlety was expected, even demanded. Sylvia felt for her but she persisted and finally the woman said, "No, it wasn't like that. If I was out someplace, I could walk wherever I needed to go. I think it was more that my brain locked up, something like that, and then my feet weren't there. Does that make sense?"

Sylvia ignored the question. None of it made sense without a larger context. "You mean you didn't feel your feet? Or just that they weren't working properly?" The woman seemed unable to answer this. Sylvia waited a moment, and then she asked, "Did you feel faint, Mrs. Simmons, or black out for any period of time when you couldn't feel your feet?"

Sylvia noticed that the questions were having a calming effect, as if, for Mrs. Simmons, the process of trying to isolate and explain her condition was a relief from worry. She was regaining color and her expression seemed less anxious. "No, I wasn't out cold or anything, just not that steady, you know?"

Sylvia nodded. "Did it affect your vision in any way?"

Mrs. Simmons looked querulous. "I can see fine. Always could. The doctor said I've got great eyes." This was clearly a point of pride, but one could never know what others would be proud of and it was useless to try.

Sylvia tried to refine the question. "Was there any cloudiness, spots in front of your eyes, or a black bar in the middle of your field of vision?"

Mrs. Simmons seemed to consider these possibilities interesting, ticking each one off on her fingers as Sylvia spoke. Then she looked at her husband and shrugged. "No, I didn't have none of that."

"Okay," Sylvia said. "Good." That ruled out syncope for the most part. She looked at the husband now. "Mr. Simmons, could you get up for a moment and let your wife sit on that stool?"

The man looked suspicious. "I'm staying in here," he said truculently.

Sylvia smiled. The husband was important. Not as important as the patient, but you didn't just treat patients; you treated families. "Of course," she said. "I didn't mean that you should leave the room. I'd just like you to let your wife sit on the stool for a while, please." The man hesitated but finally got up to let his wife take his place on the stool.

When the patient was seated, Sylvia took Mrs. Simmons by the shoulders and quickly spun her around. "Hey, what's going on?" Mr. Simmons said.

Sylvia ignored him. "Now, stand up," she commanded.

When the woman did, she staggered into her husband who had to strain to hold her erect. After Mrs. Simmons had steadied herself, Sylvia asked, "Was that the kind of dizziness you were talking about?"

It was a standard clinical maneuver, an attempt to replicate what the patient was feeling and it had the desired effect. Mrs. Simmons looked addled but she smiled hesitantly as if she was pleased with her performance. "Yes, I think it was sort of like that," she said thoughtfully, looking at the stool as if it had caused all this.

Sylvia nodded again. Vestibular dysfunction could mean a great many things, but at least they were narrowing things down. Which was the point of the differential diagnosis. You began with a wide range of illnesses to rule out.

But Mr. Simmons had had enough. "So what does she have?" he asked abruptly. "What the hell is it?"

The man acted as if Sylvia were holding out on them, though her motives for doing so would be mysterious. "I don't know if Mrs. Simmons has anything," she repeated. "You're asking me to say what something is before I know if there is anything."

"Then why are we here?" the husband asked.

It was a reasonable question. Sylvia didn't blame him for being annoyed. But it could take months to arrive at a firm diagnosis. In the meantime it was important for her to try to maintain an alliance not only with the patient but with her husband, no matter how impatient or rude he might be. "We're here to find out if there's anything wrong with your wife, and if so, what it is," she said. "By talking to you and Mrs. Simmons today I've been able to rule out some things it might have been but isn't, and I now know what she means when she says she's been dizzy."

"That's something then," Mr. Simmons said hopefully.

"Actually, it's a lot for the first examination," Sylvia said, "but this is going to go on for a while. I don't want to mislead you into thinking we're going to know something in a week or two weeks. I don't know when I'll know what's bothering your wife. I'll certainly have to see Mrs. Simmons several more times to find out more, and we'll probably run some tests on her as well. You can make an appointment outside at the desk."

Back in her office, Sylvia put in a call to her husband, but Philip was still out. He had told her he needed blocks of time in order to clarify his thinking about a scholarly project he was working on, a study of a forgotten 17th Century poet. As far as Sylvia could tell, all Philip did during these periods was smoke small cigars and go for long walks. He had actually said he was thinking of writing a book on walking as an aesthetic activity, but she wasn't sure she believed him. Still, her husband's ability to take himself seriously amazed Sylvia, especially since she now admitted privately that she didn't, hadn't for five years. She didn't admire him or what he professed to believe, nor did she respect the projects he worked on, and she resented his spending their money on trips to academic conferences and walking tours which, for reasons known only to him, always needed to be undertaken in solitary splendor. A bare three weeks after the birth of their daughter Philip had flown off to England for some conference, pleading the necessity of time and space. She was the one who had needed time and space. She was in her last year of residency and had two small children to care for.

Yet, she had not made the case then, had smiled and sent her husband off even as she was wishing that he would know what she was feeling, know that she needed him to be there for her, to take care of her and their home, know that she was feeling abandoned and alone. But even as Sylvia had these thoughts, she felt guilty for she knew that in part it was envy; she envied Philip not only his leisure but his relentless determination to indulge it. While she was honest with herself about this, she hadn't said anything to Philip and usually expressed her feelings through anger. She would blow up at him for his lack of financial acumen or disinterest in household projects, but it was all a screen for her unhappiness with him as a man. And it was odd, since her father certainly had been as selfish, though in a different way. How, she wondered, could the two most important men in her life have this in common when it was the single thing that bothered her most? Why hadn't she known better, and if she hadn't, was that Philip's fault? She couldn't say he'd changed. In fact, she had never known anyone who changed less than Philip or seemed more pleased with himself.

Still, there remained some affection between them and, miraculously, an occasional sexual flutter. Now, almost without thinking consciously about what she was doing, Sylvia began jotting down the differential diagnosis of a failed marriage on a prescription pad: marriage was a mistake in the first place; few common interests or values; a lack of love; a shortage of money; little free time; divergent views of the future; children; frequent conflict. She stopped. Face it, the diagnosis was many-faceted. In their case, all of the above were true, except conflict. They never fought or even raised their voices against one another. She thought that probably they should have fought more, that it would have helped them to stake out and refine their positions, but now it was too late. She couldn't change the dynamic of the relationship unilaterally after a dozen years of marriage. She looked again at what she had written. It was a start, though a start of what she wasn't sure. She turned the tablet over and went back into the examining room to see her next patient.

Mrs. Simmons' dizziness did not disappear and the results of Sylvia's physical examination were inconclusive. The woman wasn't dizzy constantly, after all, nor had the spells worsened to the point that she was unable to live a normal life. Mrs. Simmons could go out by herself, to shop and visit friends, and she certainly did not need someone with her at all times. There was, as far as tests could show, neither carcinoma nor pathologic vertigo. And as Sylvia ruled things out and discussed the possibilities with the family, Mr. Simmons seemed to grow more cheerful, though his wife was still morose.

"That's another one down, Doc," he said when Sylvia met with the couple one dark Monday.

"Yes, Mr. Simmons. Your wife doesn't have cancer. We can say that for sure."

"And that's good, right?"

Sylvia agreed, though somewhat more cautiously than Mr. Simmons might have liked. It was always good not to have cancer, but since the symptoms had not disappeared or lessened, she was more convinced than before that something was seriously wrong. "I'm still concerned about your wife continuing to have problems," she said. "I had hoped this might resolve spontaneously."

"Maybe she's just tired," Mr. Simmons said sympathetically. "Those kids would give anyone a run for her money."

Sylvia nodded, but she knew this wasn't exhaustion. It wasn't a transient condition. "I'd like to do some more tests," she said.

Mrs. Simmons started crying silently but her husband seemed to take Sylvia's comment as an insult. "You doctors aren't ever satisfied until you find something, are you? Even if there's nothing there, which is what you just said."

Sylvia couldn't let this pass. "That's not what I said, Mr. Simmons. I said Mrs. Simmons doesn't have cancer; she doesn't. But I do think there *is* something there. We just don't know what it is yet." There was no point in going further, in telling them what she knew to be the truth: that diseases of the central nervous system could often produce dizziness but were resistant to clear diagnosis. It took CT scans or lumbar punctures, painful and unpleasant procedures. And it took time.

Sometimes she thought of it as a problem of focus, like trying to pick out a single flower from a bouquet. She had to narrow her vision to the exclusion of everything else in order to know what she was really looking at. But Sylvia didn't explain this to Mr. Simmons because she doubted the efficacy of similes with him. Illness, while frequently fascinating to doctors and scientists, was unavoidably tragic and frustrating for patients and their families, and Sylvia accepted this along with their periodic resentment. While she cared for her patients, she also needed to see them in clinical terms as objects of study, a functional psychosis that sometimes bothered her. Mrs. Simmons' dizziness was idiopathic—nothing seemed to have caused it directly—but it wasn't temporary. Eventually, the disease, whatever it was, would declare itself in some way, and when that happened, she would have to do what she could to treat it.

Meanwhile, it did her no good to have her patient's husband suspect her. Sylvia took Mrs. Simmons' hand and palpated the cold, rigid fingers gently. "It will be all right," she said. "We'll find out what's going on. Don't worry."

Mrs. Simmons' face was blue with white patches around her nose. Water stood in her eyes. "Do you really think so?"

"I do," Sylvia said and patted her patient's arm. "It will just take some more time." But in this instance, she was afraid time would not be reassuring.

Sylvia did not really know if Philip was happy and she seldom thought about it. She came from a family of doctors who valued money and property above all else, so she had sought out a man who had no interest in such matters, an intellectual who disdained the pursuit of worldly things. Now, however, she found herself feeling resentful of her husband's lack of financial know-how, of his fussiness when it came to taking care of the cars or even shoveling the walk. It wasn't as simple as wanting him to behave more like a man, but that was certainly part of it. She may not have wanted to marry her father—an overweight obstetrician who got drunk every night and fell asleep in front of the television—but she hadn't wanted to marry her mother either. Complicating all this in Sylvia's mind was what she considered to be the impossibility of mentioning this to Philip, who thought of himself as an aesthete and wanted nothing more than to live what he seriously called the life of the mind. Sylvia didn't know where to go with that, but she wondered if part of the problem might be that the opinions of others, including those closest to him, hardly mattered to Philip. There was a curious insularity to him, she thought. No matter how foolish others' ideas were, she thought they should matter, as her patients' misguided suspicions mattered to her. And despite her elaborate defenses, she thought now of Thomas Morris, so much more accomplished than her husband but in his own way so much more modest. And it had to be said, more interested in her. Of course their relationship was unequal, she was Thomas' doctor; he was dependent on her. But the fact that a reasonably well-known concert artist would admire her more than her own husband made a difference, even if she would never act on it, never let Thomas know that he was in her thoughts. And even Philip's insensitivity to others would have been acceptable, had she not also felt that he gave her little emotionally. She rationalized that he might simply have very little to give her, and that therefore one couldn't blame him for being limited, but that didn't make it any easier to be married to the man.

On summer evenings, after the dinner dishes had been cleared and the children put to bed, they would sit on the back porch in the half-hour before bedtime, drinking tea and talking. The conversation had never been particularly stimulating, but previously Sylvia had always enjoyed these evenings. It was comfortable there in the darkness. It seemed like a reward of some kind for the difficulty of the day. And while Philip had never been especially exciting or stimulating, he had been companionable; they had been companions and now they weren't. Not really. Tonight, they were repeating the ritual, as if repetition itself could confer meaning. Yet somehow it felt perfunctory, as if each were afraid to speak openly, though Sylvia thought it was really worse than this: the truth was they had nothing to say to each other.

In the half-light, she studied her husband in profile. He was neither tall nor short, with small, squinty eyes behind wire-rimmed glasses, and a nervous mouth. He had a high forehead made ridiculous by a maginot line of hair plugs he had had inserted the year before. Philip had been quite pleased with the treatment and took the opportunity to indulge in some silk Italian shirts which he wore with ascots of various colors. While the plugs did give him the hairline he'd lacked for ten years, even a gentle breeze could disturb Philip's pompadour, leaving hair in his face and a pink scalp exposed. Sylvia had thought of suggesting that he shave it close to the scalp, but in his own way Philip was quite vain, so she had said nothing, knowing that the improvement would be minimal in any event. Often the best strategy was simply to turn away. Not that age hadn't affected her, of course, but Sylvia didn't have to be sexually attracted to herself. Tonight, for reasons she didn't know, she asked, "Are you happy?"

Philip didn't reply immediately but she knew he had heard because he started polishing his glasses furiously, a sure sign that he was thinking. Finally, he replied, "Happy? What do you mean? In what sense?"

It was hopeless. Sylvia drained her cup and rose to her feet. "Forget it," she said. "I'm just tired."

"No," Philip said. "I'm interested. Tell me what you mean."

Sylvia didn't have the energy for an intellectual discussion and was sorry now that she had said anything. "I meant exactly what I said. Are you happy?"

Now Philip smiled a lazy smile, as if this was a trick question and the answer was elusive but worth pursuing. The uncertainty was gone; he was the professor, in his element. He replaced his glasses and turned to face her. "Do I seem happy to you?"

"I don't know," Sylvia said. "That's why I asked." The truth was he didn't seem much of anything to her. Neither happy nor unhappy, neither excited nor lethargic, neither up nor down. He seemed nothing; a cipher, which was an awful thing to say or even think of her husband, and she knew it. Though if Philip were unhappy, Sylvia had no idea what his grievances against her might be.

"It's hard to know," Philip said, warming to his subject. "One must first define happiness, I suppose, before deciding if it's something that's achievable in life."

Which clinched it for Sylvia. An overwhelming weariness took possession of her. "I'm going to bed," she said, leaving Philip looking disappointed that a conversation that had seemed so promising had inexplicably come to an abrupt end.

The Simmonses were again in Sylvia's office, though now a brother in a nylon cap advertising a trucking company had joined his sister and her husband. Time for some answers, Sylvia figured; she only wished she had more of them.

"The results of the CT scan and Mrs. Simmons' MRI are back," she began.

Mr. Simmons took his wife's hand, steeling himself for the worst, though it wasn't clear what the worst would be in his mind. But before Sylvia could go on, the brother spoke in a husky growl. "I got a friend at work's got that Lou Gehrig disease," he said. "Started out just like Molly."

It was a relief to be able to give them relatively good news. "I'm certain Mrs. Simmons isn't suffering from ALS," Sylvia said, and the family seemed visibly relieved. It was always useful to know what patients feared, especially since in most cases it had nothing to do with their actual condition. Generally, they worried about cancer or brain tumors or heart disease, but seldom about Huntington's chorea or Reiter's syndrome, which in their own unique ways were worse. Sylvia's job was often that of educator, but her subject was always the horrific.

"And it's not that AIDS we're always hearing about, is it?" The way Mr. Simmons asked the question indicated this was his real fear, though Sylvia was certain that his wife's dizziness had nothing to do with sexually transmitted diseases.

"Absolutely not," Sylvia said, and she could feel the sigh of relief. Having gotten their fantasies out of the way, she spread the plastic film on the viewing screen on her office wall, hoping to explain or at least demonstrate some of the findings. "These solid areas are plaques," she said, indicating some murky gray areas. Mr. Simmons pulled glasses from the pocket of his work shirt and edged closer. She felt the brother's warm breath on her shoulder and moved slightly to the side. They both looked at her for further enlightenment.

"That's not normal," Sylvia said, making things as simple as possible. "It indicates some trauma to Mrs. Simmons' nervous system."

"Seems pretty calm most of the time," her brother observed. "She has her issues, but mostly she ain't nervous."

It was interesting to Sylvia that such a man would use a word like issues, but everyone listened to talk shows now, so perhaps she shouldn't have been surprised. "I didn't mean that Mrs. Simmons is nervous," she continued. "Everyone has a nervous system. It controls the brain and most of our bodily functions."

The Simmonses nodded in unison, not wishing to argue, intimidated by the film Sylvia had mounted on the wall. Mrs. Simmons had not yet spoken. "What's it mean then?" Mr. Simmons said.

"Unfortunately, I'm not sure about that," Sylvia said. "The presence of the nervous system is what's common; the plaques I showed you aren't."

"Not sure," Mr. Simmons exploded. "I'd like you to tell me something you *are* sure about for once. We're coming down here, what, six weeks now, and you're poking and examining and driving my poor wife crazy, and now she's inside that goddamned tube for forty-five minutes scared out of her wits, and you still don't know why she's falling down in our kitchen. What kind of doctor are you anyway?"

"Not a very good one in your opinion, I'm sure," Sylvia said. But she was grateful for his anger. Why shouldn't he be outraged? Even if she knew that good health was a gift that people took for granted as long as it lasted, it was maddening to be suddenly affected as his wife had been, and to know so little about her illness or its course. And while doctors might find it intellectually challenging to ferret out the diagnosis eventually through trial and error, it was ruining the Simmonses' lives. "I do have some ideas," she said, trying to reassure them. "And the tests did help. We're getting closer to finding out what's wrong. I'm sorry I can't be more definite."

As quickly as Mr. Simmons' anger had erupted, it now subsided. "It's okay," he said. "It's not your fault, I know that. It's no one's fault. But the thing is for years she's just fine, waking up early, taking care of me and the kids, making our meals, doing the laundry and housework. Then, before you know it, she's on her keyster, too tired to butter bread. Takes your breath away, I'll tell you, how quick it came."

"Some diseases are like that," Sylvia said. "They just appear for no apparent reason."

"But it's real, right?" the brother put in. "I read in *Reader's Digest* some people ain't really sick, even if they can't work and all."

"You're probably talking about Chronic Fatigue Syndome," Sylvia said. "But this is real, I can guarantee you that, even if I don't know for sure what it is." It was important that they know this. The last thing Mrs. Simmons needed was her family thinking she was malingering. "In a few weeks I'll be able to tell you more, but I believe Mrs. Simmons has a neurological illness, which means her falling is unrelated to trauma or a tumor."

"She don't have cancer then?" Mr. Simmons said.

"No," Sylvia said patiently. "We've ruled that out." Who the "we" was exactly was uncertain, even to her. Dr. Peters, the referring physician was out of this now, and the faceless laboratory technicians who processed film were usually unable to interpret their own work. She was in this alone, trying to make it all understandable and somewhat less frightening to her patient.

For the first time, Mrs. Simmons spoke. "That's what I was worried about, to tell the truth. I guess I can live with anything else."

"Okay," the brother said, summing up. "She don't have cancer and she don't have AIDS or Lou Gehrig's?"

"Yes," Sylvia said. "I've already told you that."

The family took this as good news. Mr. Simmons and his brother-in-law slapped palms and relaxed into their chairs. In a sense they were right, but given the range of diseases Mrs. Simmons might have, Sylvia was not encouraged. She often said in a joking way to friends: if you come to see me, there's a good chance you're really sick. It was a bad joke, but true. Sometimes she hated how true it was. Now she allowed the Simmonses to think the worst had been ruled out because it was easier for her, and she was ashamed of this.

"Well, all right then, Doctor," Mr. Simmons said. "We'll see you later."

Sylvia smiled in response, but there would come a time when she would have an answer for them and she was reasonably sure that no one would be smiling then.

Sylvia had found a sealed letter from Philip on the breakfast table that morning, but she hadn't had the time or will to read it. Now she took the single sheet out of the envelope and spread it before her on the desk. It seemed to be in response to their aborted talk about happiness of the night before, though Philip didn't address that directly. Instead, he had made a list, headed "What I Need From a Woman." Sylvia noted the indefinite article, and then she read what her husband had written.

1.) A willingness to share in my life and concerns.
2.) Support for my work.
3.) To be a partner in every sense.
4.) A love of the natural world equal to my own.
5.) Sensitivity to the arts and literature.
6.) Commitment to social/political issues.
7.) Spirituality.

Sylvia went through the list twice, noting that it was Philip's life, work, and politics that needed to be supported; apparently the woman in question was to have none, or perhaps she was misunderstanding his intentions. Maybe the appropriate response would now be to supply Philip with her own list. Then they could collate the two lists and negotiate a final document which they could each sign, like a treaty or formal agreement.

She wasn't sure whether this was a reaction to her question about happiness or something he'd been thinking about on his own for some time. In either case, the whole thing was so pathetic as an attempt at communication that she wanted to laugh, but it was obvious that Philip expected some kind of reply.

She sat back in her chair, wondering how they had gotten to this point, but she could think of nothing, no root cause, no developing problems that she should have attended to earlier. Their marriage hadn't started out this way and neither of them had intended for things to develop as they had, but here they were. What was wrong with their marriage was idiopathic, like Mrs. Simmons' dizziness, and it had about as much chance of successful intervention. She looked again at the list and shook her head. Then she started arranging her things for the afternoon carpool. She checked her list of patients for the following day, and then, in the margin of her calendar, wrote: "Call lawyer." ❧

In The End

Robert Nazarene

In the end

      (if this is

       the end)

I will meet

you at the

end of what

you think is

the end

      ℘

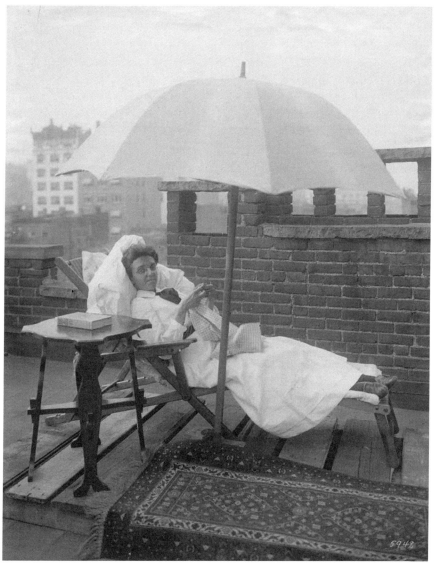

Home treatment of TB, circa 1909. Photographer: Jessie Tarbox Beals. Courtesy of Bellevue Hospital Archives: Chest Collection. Beals (1870-1942) was the first woman photojournalist. A self-taught photographer, she was known for "capturing the soul" of New York City. It is not entirely clear how she came to photograph Bellevue and its patients, but her photos span 1906-1938. Though she was commercially successful, illness and the Great Depression took their toll and she died penniless, ironically, in a charity ward at Bellevue Hospital, possibly of TB. (Other Beals photos on pages 23 and 126.)

Contributors' Notes

Jan Lee Ande's first book, *Instructions for Walking on Water,* winner of the 2000 Snyder Award, was published by Ashland Poetry Press. Her second book, *Reliquary,* won the 2002 X.J. Kennedy Prize and was published by Texas Review Press. Her poems appear in *New Letters, Image, Mississippi Review, Notre Dame Review, Nimrod,* and *Poetry International.* She teaches poetry, ecopoetics, and history of religions at Union Institute & University.

Priscilla Atkins was born and raised in central Illinois. She holds degrees from Smith College and the University of Hawaii. Her work has appeared in such journals as *Poetry, The North American Review, The Laurel Review,* and *Passages North.* She has taught elementary school and served in the Poets-in-the-Schools program on Oahu; currently she is the arts librarian at Hope College, in Holland, Michigan.

Daniel C. Bryant graduated from the College of Physicians and Surgeons at Columbia University in 1965 and practiced internal medicine in Portland, Maine until retirement in 1999. His poems have been published in both medical journals and literary magazines. *Home Free* is Daniel's first published work of fiction. He has created a web site profiling nearly 400 physician writers (http://members.aol.com/dbryantmd/index.html).

Michael Casey's first book, *Obscenities,* was in the Yale Younger Poet Series in 1972. His later books are *Millrat* (Adastra Press, 1999) and *The Million Dollar Hole* (Orchises Press, 2001). He teaches at the University of Massachusetts at Lowell and Northern Essex Community College.

Megan Corazza is a recent graduate of Whitman College, where she majored in Asian Studies and completed a pre-medical program. She spent a year in Nepal volunteering at a medical clinic, studying tuberculosis and interviewing traditional healers. Currently Megan is building a log cabin and coaching high school cross-country skiing in Homer, Alaska. In the summers she runs a commercial fishing boat.

Sharon Dolin is the author of *Heart Work* (Sheep Meadow). Her collection of ekphrastic poems, *Serious Pink,* has just been published this spring by Marsh Hawk Press, and another book of poems, *Realm of the Possible,* will be published by Four Way Books in 2004. She teaches poetry workshops at the Unterberg Poetry Center of the 92nd St. Y and is the Coordinator and Co-judge of The Center for Book Arts Annual Letterpress Poetry Chapbook Competition.

Steve Fayer's story, *Parricide*, appeared in the Fall 2001 *Bellevue Literary Review.* Recently he has also published fiction in *Potpourri, The Potomac Review, Jewish Currents,* and *New York Stories.* Fayer is co-author of *Voices Of Freedom,* a history of the civil rights movement (Bantam, 1990). As a writer for PBS, he received an Emmy for *Mississippi: Is This America?,* a part of the *Eyes On The Prize* series, and a Writers' Guild of America Award for *George Wallace: Settin' The Woods On Fire.*

Erica Funkhouser's fourth book of poetry, *Pursuit,* was published by Houghton Mifflin in 2002. She teaches Poetry Writing at MIT and lives in Essex, MA.

Meghan Hickey's poems are published or forthcoming in *The Cream City Review, Harvard Review, The Larcom Review, Borderlands: Texas Poetry Review,* and *The Saint Ann's Review.* She lives and works in New Jersey.

Susan Ito is the coeditor of *A Ghost at Heart's Edge: Stories & Poems of Adoption,* a literary collection published by North Atlantic Books. Her work has appeared in many journals and anthologies, including *The Readerville Journal, Hip Mama, Making More Waves,* and *Growing Up Asian American.* She lives in Oakland, California with her family.

Jesse Lee Kercheval is the author of the poetry collection, *World as Dictionary,* and the memoir, *Space.* Her new collection, *Dog Angel,* is forthcoming from the University of Pittsburgh Press. She teaches at the University of Wisconsin-Madison, where she directs their new MFA program.

Sandra Kohler's poems have appeared in magazines including *The New Republic, Prairie Schooner, The Gettysburg Review, The Colorado Review, Elixir,* and *The Southern Review.* Her first book of poems, *The Country of Women,* was published by Calyx in 1995. Her second book, *The Ceremonies of Longing,* is the winner of the 2002 AWP Award Series in Poetry, and will be published by the University of Pittsburgh Press. She lives and writes in Selinsgrove, a small town on the Susquehanna River in Central Pennsylvania.

Sheila Kohler is the author of four novels: *The Perfect Place*, *The House on R Street*, *Cracks*, and *Children of Pithiviers*, and two collections of short stories: *Miracles in America* and *One Girl*. Kohler has been awarded the O. Henry, the Open Voice, and the Smart Family Foundation prizes, as well as the Willa Cather Prize, judged by William Gass, for *One Girl*.

Itzhak Kronzon has published over seventy short stories in Israeli (and recently, American) journals, newspapers, and magazines, including the Fall 2001 *Bellevue Literary Review*. Two books—*Mother, Sunshine, Homeland* (1985) and *Who Will Get Belgium* (1991)—were published in Hebrew in his native Israel. He is a cardiologist and Professor of Medicine at NYU School of Medicine, as well as Senior Professor at Tel Aviv University, and Director and Consultant at Escorts Heart Institute in New Delhi, India.

Marylee MacDonald, a former restoration carpenter, is the editor of *River Oak Review*, a Chicago literary magazine. Her fiction and nonfiction have been published in *StoryQuarterly*, *Four Quarters*, and *River Oak Review* as well as a number of national consumer and trade publications. In 2000, she was an Illinois Arts Council Finalist, and she received an Illinois Arts Council Fellowship in 2001.

H. L. McNaugher has had fiction and poetry in *Blithe House Quarterly*, *The 12th Street Review*, *Beacon Street Review*, and *Anteup*. She is currently pursuing a doctorate in English at SUNY Binghamton.

David Milofsky is the author of three novels, and his fourth book, *A Friend of Kissinger*, will be published in the spring of 2003. His short stories, articles, and reviews have appeared in a variety of publications, including *Prairie Schooner*, *The New York Times*, *The New York Times Magazine*, and elsewhere. He has twice won grants from the NEA and currently is Professor of English at Colorado State University where he edits the *Colorado Review* and serves as director of the Center for Literary Publishing.

Robert Nazarene's poetry has appeared or is forthcoming in *Crazyhorse*, *The Oxford American*, *Ploughshares*, *Quarterly West*, and elsewhere. He is a graduate of the McDonough School of Business at Georgetown University and is founding editor of *Margie / The American Journal of Poetry*.

Natalie Pearson completed her MFA in Nonfiction Writing at the University of Iowa in December, 2002. She has worked as a teacher, reporter, and editor. Her stories and essays have been published in regional magazines and news-papers, as well as in *Salon* and *Writers Write*. She also writes essays aired on public radio.

Simon Perchik is an attorney whose poetry has appeared in *Partisan Review, The Nation, New Yorker,* and elsewhere. His books include *Hands Collected* (Pavement Saw Press, 2000), *Touching the Headstone* (Stride Publications, 2000), and *The Autochthon Poems* (Split/Shift, 2001).

Joan Reibman is Associate Professor of Medicine and Physiology in the Division of Pulmonary & Critical Care Medicine at NYU School of Medicine and Bellevue Hospital. In 2000, she delivered a lecture on tuberculosis and writers at the Nobel Symposium on TB in Stockholm, Sweden.

Linda Goodman Robiner's chapbook, *Reverse Fairy Tale*, was published by Pudding House. More than 220 of her poems as well as five short stories have been published. She has taught at Notre Dame College, Cuyahoga Community College, Ursuline College, Cleveland State University, and John Carroll University. She delights in facilitating writing workshops.

Ruthann Robson's work discussing her cancer experience has recently appeared in *Creative Nonfiction, Another Chicago Magazine, Harvard Gay & Lesbian Review, Out,* and *Self.* She is the author of several works of fiction including the novel *A/K/A* (St. Martin's Press, 1998) and many works on legal issues of interest to lesbians including *Sappho Goes To Law School* (Columbia University Press 1998). She is Professor of Law at the City University of New York School of Law.

Clarence Smith is in his third year of medical school at Vanderbilt University. He has a short story forthcoming in *Rosebud*.

James Tate, winner of the Pulitzer Prize and the National Book Award, has also won Guggenheim and NEA Fellowships, the Tanning Prize from the Academy of American Poets, and the William Carlos Williams Award. His first book of poems, *The Lost Pilot*, won the Yale Younger Poets series award in 1967. His most recent collection is *Lost River* (Sarabande Books, 2003).

Jim Tolan's poems have appeared or are forthcoming in *American Literary Review, Atlanta Review, Indiana Review, International Quarterly, Louisiana Literature, Luna, Many Mountains Moving, Margie, Salt Hill, Windsor Review,* and *Wisconsin Review,* among others. He runs Tuesday Nights at The Muddy Cup, a poetry series in Staten Island.

Abraham Verghese is Professor of Medicine and the director of The Center for Medical Humanities and Ethics at University of Texas School of Medicine at San Antonio. His first book, *My Own Country,* about a doctor's struggle with the new AIDS epidemic, was a finalist for the National Book Critics Circle Award for 1994 and was the basis for a movie. His second book, *The Tennis Partner,* was a New York Times notable book and a national bestseller. His writing has appeared in *The New Yorker, The Atlantic Monthly, Esquire, Granta, The New York Times Magazine,* and elsewhere. He is currently completing a novel.

Kristin Camitta Zimet is the author of *Take in My Arms the Dark,* a collection of poems published by the Sow's Ear Press in 1999. She works as a nature guide in the Shenandoah Valley of Virginia.

Acknowledgements

The *Bellevue Literary Review* would like to express its deep gratitude to all who have helped support the journal in its efforts to bridge the worlds of literature and medicine.

Publisher: Lenox Hill Hospital

Benefactors: Dr. Salvatore V. Ambrosino, H. Dale & Elizabeth Hemmerdinger, Rita J. & Stanley H. Kaplan Family Foundation Inc., Dr. George D. Mitchell, Drs. Anthony & Elayne Mustalish, Edith Rathbun, Billie & Laurence Tisch, Dr. Bradley J. Wechsler

Muses: Dr. Cori Baill, Mr. & Mrs. Fred Lee Barber, Dr. Ira Breite & Dr. Sandy Zabar, William Lee Frost, Dr. Edwin S. Gardiner, Sylvia Hassenfeld, Dr. Katherine Matthews, Dr. Franco Muggia, Dr. Adam S. Rubenstein

Friends: Dr. Doreen Addrizzo-Harris, Dr. Louise Aronson, Dr. L. Fred Ayvazian, Dr. Louis J. Capponi, Dr. A. Bernice Clark, Dr. David C. Ferris, Lola Finkelstein, Dr. Alec Goldenberg, Silvia Hafliger, Drs. William & Mary Houghton, Dr. Franklin Jackson, Dr. Martin L. Kahn, Kashdan/Ofri family, Abram E. Kirschenbaum, Arlene & Richard Kossoff, Dr. Edith J. Langner, Robin Lifton, Dr. Mark S. Lipton, Dr. Robert Maslansky, Dr. Eric Neilson, Eleanor & Gerald Piel, Dr. Jeffrey M. Shapiro, Dr. William Slater & Dr. Veronica Catanese, Naomi & Robert Spira, Ronald J. Stein, Gilbert Tauber, Dr. William C. Taylor, Staffan Wahlander, Robert Warshaw

Supporters: Janet Jeppson Asimov, Martin Baier, Dr. Frances Bailen-Rose, Richard J. Baron, Daniel M. Becker, Aaron Beckerman, Laura Boylan, Dr. Lynn Buckvar-Keltz, Dr. Louis A. Buzzeo, Dr. Alan J. Coleman, Dr. Charles Debrovner, John Deeley, Phillip Dibble, Dr. Daniel G. Duke, Bernard Ehrlich, Dr. Jonathan Florman, Diana Forbes, Dr. Stephen A. Geller, Dan George, Dr. Charles Hazzi, Charles S. Hirsch, Margaret A. Jacobs, Dr. Sandra Kammerman, Dr. Arthur Lebowitz, Bernice L. Lewis, Dr. Arthur E. Lindner, Jodi Donetta Lowry, Dr. Leonard Meiselas, Mercy College, Harry Naidich, Neal Neuman, Northside Hospital, Dr. Peter M. Palese, Dr. William Schaffner, Dr. Mark D. Schwartz & Dr. Adina Kalet, Suzanne R. Simon, Ellen S. Sleight, Dr. Norton Spritz, Dr. Lloyd Wasserman, Carol West, Mieko Willoughby

Folio

A Literary Journal

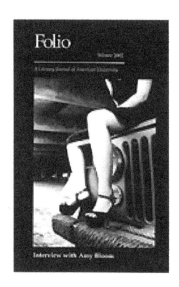

Subscriptions

$12 / 1 year (2 issues)
$24 / 2 years (4 issues)
Sample copies available for $6

Submission Guidelines

Folio looks for work that ignites and endures, is artful and natural, daring and elegant. Manuscripts are read between September 1 and March 1. Please send no more than 5 poems or 3,500 words of double-spaced prose per submission.

Submissions should include a cover letter with your name, address, phone number, and e-mail address. Also please include a brief bio, title(s) of work enclosed, and an SASE.

Department of Literature
American University
Washington, DC 20016
folio_editors@yahoo.com